FROM CRACK TO COLLEGE
AND VICE VERSA

MARILYN D. JONES, M.ED.

"I freed a thousand slaves. I could have freed a thousand more if only they knew they were slaves."

Harriet Tubman

Prelude

I wish I could tell you the reasons why you should read this book, but I can't because there is no telling what you may get out of it. I have allowed an audience of diverse readers, including scholars, active and recovering addicts, social workers, choice family members and choice friends, to read portions of this book prior to publishing, and everybody walked away with different messages. To keep it real with you, I knew I had something that was worth putting out there when an active crack addict stayed up all night reading this.

I realize that I may subject myself to ridicule, but I am not worried. It is what it is. This is MY life story. I am not proud of MANY aspects of it, and I am not sure why it must be made public, but it is something I feel compelled to do. It has been over four years since I wrote the majority of this book, and I wrote things back then that I wouldn't have necessarily written today. However, when I wrote this book, I had approximately 60 days crack-free, and I was feeling the wrath of crack cocaine a lot more than I am right now. Nevertheless, I feel it is important to tell the story as I saw fit back then.

I have tried to protect people who may be subject to sudden cases of amnesia or be otherwise offended by the truth by changing their names or by not giving them a name at all. Unfortunately, I was unable to incorporate a rationale for many of my actions during my life without elaborating on my childhood. That was the part of this book that was the hardest to write, but without writing that part I would have presented myself as someone who just went sour for no reason, so the story had to be told from the beginning. This is something God wants me to do, so it is done.

I cannot lie; this is NOT a tell all. There are some things that I choose to keep between God and myself. However, I want you to know that I really put myself out there when I wrote this book because my hopes were and still are that someone will read this book and be empowered to make a positive change in their life or look at certain people they have been judging adversely in a more compassionate manner.

This book is dedicated to my praying grandmother, Mai Mai. (God rest her soul.) I am truly sorry for any undue suffering I may have caused you. You were my rock and anchor; without your understanding and LOVE, I would be nothing. This book is also dedicated to all of my children (I know it may be hard for you to read this), my granddaughters, my grandchildren to come, and finally, my first cousin, Robyn, who has been my support system throughout the years. In addition, this book is dedicated to the massive number of crack cocaine casualties in the Black community, meaning those who have been locked up, smoked out, or lost their lives due to crack cocaine; I have not forgotten about you.

I would also like to give a shout out to my English teacher, Mr. Langdon. You were very instrumental in helping me to realize my capabilities, and you also edited my book for free. Whenever this book blows up,

I am going to look out for you. THAT'S A PROMISE. This book derived from an English assignment that you gave me to write about my life. It started out as seven pages, but I realized that it was worth telling. Thank you so much!

Chapter One: The Closet

At the age of 20, I had been on crack cocaine for approximately six months when an elderly woman asked me with a disgusted look on her face, "Have you looked in the mirror lately?" Later on that day, I took a good look in the mirror, and I must admit that it saddened me. I guess I hadn't looked in the mirror for at least six months, which is how long I had been on dope. As I examined myself, I first noticed that the white schoolboy shirt I had on was damn near brown, and I then realized that I hadn't changed clothes in weeks. I began to examine myself more closely and focused on the person in the mirror wearing the grimy clothes. I saw a shell that used to be my body; there were bones visible in my chest and face that I had never seen before. My hair was dry, brittle and lifeless looking, and my skin had a grey-blue tint, but the worst part was my eyes.

I saw eyes that no longer had a spark of hope; they looked like empty deep pools, but ironically my eyes were the only part of my body that resembled the old me. Somehow they were still pretty. It was really sad because my eyes seemed as if they had been kidnapped and wanted to be rescued; they began to tear up. I had to look away, so I was unable to connect with that person in the mirror. Although I was unhappy with what I saw, I was too far gone in my addiction with a lot more mileage left on my feet to make any changes. The crack wouldn't allow me to at that point. I now had another reason to smoke dope: to help me avoid myself.

Nineteen eight five was the year that I was introduced to crack cocaine. However, in order to understand the roots of my story, I have to go back further to a difficult period of time in my life. From the ages of 9 through 13, I lived with my father, my so-called stepmother, and her three children (the two boys were by my dad and the other girl was from a previous relationship) in San Mateo County. I am calling her my so-called stepmother because although she was using my father's last name, they were never married. Up until the age of nine, I had been living with my grandparents on my mother's side in a loving home that was centered around me because I was the only child in the household. My mother left me with my grandparents because she was a mere 15 years old when she gave birth to me, and I was raised in the Western Addition, a neighborhood in San Francisco, which is also known as the Fillmore (to break it down even further, Fillmoe).

Fillmoe used to be a primarily Black community in San Francisco, but that has since changed. Today Black people only represent a third of the population, and a great many of us live in public housing/low-income housing sites (mini-plantations) instead of being homeowners, as were many of the Black residents of Fillmoe when I was I was a small child. San Francisco has earned the reputation of being a very liberal and diverse city, but it is turning whiter every year. Black folks as a whole are not flourishing; we represent a mere seven percent of the general population and over sixty percent of the county jail population in San Francisco. You go do the math and tell me if this is a place that I can consider to appreciate diversity.

In the early 1970's, there was a strong Black Panther presence in Fillmoe; one of their headquarters was located on Fillmore Street. Black pride was the theme back then. Many Black people in the community were wearing big afros, *Free Angela Davis* buttons, and pumping the Black power fist in the air at a moment's notice. I may have been just a little girl during this time period, but I was oh so proud to be in my Black skin!

Back then, the vast majority of the businesses and residences in Fillmoe were Black owned. I went to John Muir Elementary School, a primarily Black school that taught African dance, and we all were expected to know the Black national anthem, "Lift Every Voice and Sing." Being Black was so in at the time that the local Black-owned ice cream parlor on Haight Street sold Black ice cream, which was vanilla ice cream dyed Black.

As you will notice, I have chosen to use the word Black instead of African-American throughout this story because when the term "African-American" was introduced the words "beautiful", "power" and "pride" were not included with the slogan, so I've decided to keep it Black BECAUSE BLACK IS STILL BEAUTIFUL.
Early in my childhood, when I was around 4-6 years old, my auntie was an active member of the Black power movement. She was just a teenager, but I watched her actions. She taught me to be proud that I was Black, and this high level of Black pride has stuck with me to this very day although sometimes it can be hard to believe that I am blessed to be Black based upon the messages I receive from society.

I can remember when I was just a little girl, and James Brown came out with the song entitled "Say it Loud." My auntie shouted, "Say it Loud!!" out of one of the front windows in the Victorian flat we were living in, and I in turn shouted out of the other window at the top of my voice, "I'm Black and I'm proud!!!" Although I was only about 4 years old at the time, that was one of the proudest moments of my life.

While I was living with my grandparents, Mai Mai and Pa Pa (pronounced May May and Paw Paw), I used to spend time visiting with my father and his family every now and then. My father's house was nice to visit, but when I moved in, it turned out to be a very abusive household. My so-called stepmother was the main one who wanted me to move in; I am not sure what her motives were. Possibly, she wanted to get on my dad's good side; however, I was abused mentally, physically and sexually in that household.

As I mentioned previously, there were three other children in the household, two boys and one girl. The girl, whom I will call Latrice, was only four months older than I was, and we became very close; we did everything together. Latrice was the only child in the household who wasn't my father's biological child. Although we were of no real relation because my father was not married to her mother, our relationship grew to be very close, and we considered ourselves sisters. The two boys were younger than I was. One was four years younger and the other was nine years younger.

This household was much different than the loving home I lived in with my grandparents. There was a lot of responsibility put on the oldest child and eventually myself. The longer I stayed, the more immoral behavior took place towards me. My so-called stepmother was pure-dee evil. Although she was the one who really petitioned for me to move from my grandparents' house, she was also the one who initiated my regular beatings. I still remember the first beating. I can't remember what I did wrong, but I wasn't allowed to go to a party, and I was beaten with an extension cord. One of the strokes went across my face and eye. I was around 10 years old at the time.

From that point on, she became more and more abusive. She spoke with Latrice and me as if we were adults. Now that I have a 10-year-old child of my own, I realize how twisted some of her conversations about her problems were. Latrice and I were literally her only friends. On a few occasions, my so-called stepmother told me when I did something that she perceived to be wrong, "That's why your mother don't want you." Those were very painful words that have stuck with me to this very day. My father was just plain strange, which I will go into more detail about further on.

We lived in a huge house in Foster City around the white folks, and my father drove the nicest cars because he worked for a car dealership, but ironically there was not much food available, which was the opposite of the situation in my grandparents' house, where I was able to eat and drink what I wanted endlessly. As a result, I would orchestrate plans to raid the refrigerator while my father and so-called stepmother slept; now that I think about it that was how I first learned to steal.

By the age of 13, I began to question certain behavior in this ridiculous, dysfunctional setting. I can clearly remember asking Latrice late one night, "Does Daddy rub on your titties?" To be honest, I can't remember her response because it has been too many years ago, and her response was too vague. The reason I asked the above-mentioned question is because my father used to ask me to come watch television with him in his bed. He pretended like he was paying attention to the television, but he would gradually start rubbing the sides of my breasts with the back of his fingers, and sometimes he would twist my earlobes with his finger and thumb. That made me feel very creepy. To this date, it creeps me out for someone to touch my earlobes, and you've got to be pretty special to touch my breasts.

A few weeks after I asked Latrice about my dad's inappropriate sexual behaviors, she was found to be seven months pregnant at the age of 13, and my dad was the sperm donor. According to Latrice, he had been sexually molesting her since the age of five, and this was not her first pregnancy. She told me that a previous pregnancy by my father was aborted when she was 11 years old, and she was instructed by him to say she was raped under the Foster City Bridge. She was my best friend in the whole wide world; I considered her blood. I felt horrible that my parent did that to her.

To my recollection, my dad never penetrated me, but he did touch me inappropriately and beat the shit out of me on a regular basis. Somehow I was able to remain defiant despite all of this; I always spoke up for myself when I was being beaten, which made the beatings worse, but I believe my rebellious personality was a trait that made him limit what he did with me sexually.   Plus, according to my dad, Pa Pa, my grandfather on my mother's side, was a gangster who was not to be fooled with.

Up until I moved in with my dad, I was what would now be considered a nerd. I read encyclopedias and books all day long, and I used to teach my grandmother and little cousin different things I learned in school on a small blackboard that my grandmother set up in my room. This type of behavior was encouraged at my grandparents' house, but books and scholastic achievement were not valued in my father's home.

Latrice was known as a good fighter, and my father and so-called stepmother were very proud of that. Up until coming to live with my father, I had only had one fight in my entire life, which was in the 3rd grade at John Muir with a boy who was picking on me. However, after I began living with my father, I began fighting regularly, showing out negatively in school, and running away from home on a regular basis. As a result, the seventh grade would be the last grade I was to complete up until I got the GED at the age of 17.

During the latter part of the four years that I lived with my dad and his family, I used to really regret when he would come home. Latrice and I would play sleep if we heard him come in, but that wouldn't help matters. He would come home in the wee hours of the mornings after gambling all night and blast the stereo that was kept in our room. Sometimes he would go as far as shooting us with water pistols to make sure we got up to make us play dominoes with him while he cracked up laughing. These domino games lasted two or three hours during the middle of the night, and my dad would always win; he called himself a dominologist.

That is just a short preview of what I had to reason with as a child living in a very stressful and unfit environment, so I began to take refuge in the closet in my room. It felt like a really safe place. There was a large walk-in closet located in the room I shared with Latrice. It was dark and quiet, and I wasn't bothered while I was in there. No one asked me to go in there, but I can remember feeling safely removed from the world, and this is where I went as soon as I got home from school.

Latrice and I weren't allowed to participate in any after school programs because we were expected to watch our little brothers immediately after school. Taking refuge in the closet went on for the last year or so I lived with my father. I really believe that the hiding I did in the closet was a significant change in my life. It represented when I learned how to check out when things became too much for me.

Because of his sexual abuse of my sister, my father was sentenced to do three months in a work furlough program. Yes, three months. For a short period of time after everything was exposed, my sister was removed from the household and lived in an unwed mother's home in Oakland, California, until her son was born. The rest of the family still lived together as if nothing happened.

Everyone was responsible for keeping the ultimate secret: my father was a child molester. One day I relayed the secret to one of my closest friends; her mother forbade me to see her anymore, and the word got out. My so-called stepmother got wind that the news had gotten outside of the family because of me, and she called me a bunch of bitches. I felt really bad for having opened my big mouth and allowing the word to get out. However, I must acknowledge that the secret was too BIG for me. I couldn't hold it then, nor can I hold it right now.

I can remember being scared to death that my so-called stepmother found out that I told the family secret. As an adult, I found out that my so-called stepmother had plans to tell the story another way when my sister and the baby came home. Many years later, Latrice told me that my so-called stepmother had concocted a story that placed herself as the new baby's mother; she was really overweight at the time and probably could have pulled it off to some degree.

Ironically, my sister was allowed to return to the home once she had her baby, and I was the baby's babysitter during the day while she attended school because I had been kicked out of middle school and the entire school district for acting out. Even though I was the primary person that watched my little brother, whom I then referred to as my nephew, my father would come home and yell at me to wash my hands when dealing with the baby. I can't clearly remember; he may have been in work furlough during this time period, but I do remember him being at the house. I watched that baby all day long, and nobody called to check on him. When my father yelled at me to wash my hands, he made me feel dirty and didn't acknowledge the fact that I was caring for his child the best I could. I was only 13 years old.

The reason why I was kicked out of school in the 8th grade is because I was fighting on a regular basis at the middle school I attended in San Mateo, and the Vice Principal, whom I shall call Mr. Pippa, got in the middle of one of the fights and claimed he got hit. Mr. Pippa couldn't stand me, so he pressed charges against me for assault. However, when the police came to my door and read me my rights, they realized that I was only four feet eleven inches tall, and Mr. Pippa, who was over six feet tall, was not suffering from any injuries. If Mr. Pippa had, had it his way, I would have been arrested.

The police didn't pursue the charges pressed against me, but Mr. Pippa still made sure that I was not allowed to come back to school even though I met with him and practically begged him to let me back in. Not once did any school officials try to figure out why I was acting the way I was, nor did any agencies seek to remove me from this situation although it was known that my father was a convicted pedophile. Instead, I was made to feel as if I was a bad child.

I guess my father couldn't deal with the situation after everything was exposed, so he made arrangements for the house to be sold. For a period of time (exactly how long I can't recall for the life of me), my so-called stepmother was gone from the house, and my father and I were in the home alone. I was looking through some drawers while my dad and I were preparing to move stuff out of the house and found open letters that my biological mother had written to me that I believe my so-called stepmother had been hiding. All of this time my so-called stepmother led me to believe that my mother didn't care about me at all; a STRONG hatred was born for her that day.

The letters from my biological mom weren't very deep in content. Basically, my mother was just writing to let me know she cared, and in one letter she asked if I needed anything and offered to give me an allowance. Although the letters weren't what I would consider to be deep, I can clearly remember the beautiful handwriting my mother had. I had never seen such beautiful handwriting like that before. I wanted to write like that, so I studied her handwriting and learned how to write like her. To this day, my handwriting looks very much like my mother's.

If I had known that my mother actually did care about me, I would have told her how I was being treated. My mother would have helped if she had known. Instead, I just dealt with it. I was afraid, and I didn't think I had anyone who could help me. I was just a baby in a terrible situation. Sometimes I wish I had said something; maybe my sister wouldn't have suffered at the hands of my father for so long. I was also afraid to tell my grandmother because I believed something would happen to her; my so-called stepmother had me scared to death. Now that I am grown, I wish that I had spoken up. I now realize that people did love me, and I should have asked for help.

Believe it or not, my father was not only sleeping with my sister, but he also had a relationship with a woman he met on his job. I'm not sure if he started messing with her before or after the sexual abuse was exposed. My father's new girlfriend was only eight years older than I was, and she could not stand me. Nevertheless, I lived with her for a brief period while my dad completed his three-month work furlough sentence. My father's girlfriend and I constantly argued, and she would call the police on me to try to have me removed from the household.

The police told her that they couldn't take me anywhere for just arguing and that I would have to do something to her for them to take me into custody, and they left. That very same day my father's girlfriend re-called the police on me. She kept on picking on me, and she swung open the door in the bedroom that I was sleeping in. Irritated by this treatment, I tried to slam the bedroom door back, and that was all she needed to be able to re-call the police and say I hit her with the door. I was then taken to juvenile hall, where I stayed for one month and twenty days. I'll never forget the amount of time I spent there. It was overwhelming and uncalled for.

I was taken to San Mateo County Juvenile Hall, which was then referred to as Hillcrest. One thing that made my situation complicated is that I was pregnant when I got arrested. At the age of 14, I got pregnant by a boy that I met at a party that my father gave me permission to go to for a couple of hours. I left the party with the boy, we had sex, and I got pregnant as a result. (My so-called stepmother put out the rumor that the baby was my father's, but that was not true. As far as I can remember, my father never penetrated me.)

When I first got to Hillcrest, I was extremely mad and would throw temper tantrums. I can't remember why, but I do remember having my socks and shoes pulled off and being literally dragged to the hole, solitary confinement. I stayed there for a week or two. I could have gotten out sooner, but every time the juvenile staff came to talk to me, I cussed them out. I was angry, and they didn't try to figure out why; again, I was made to believe I was just a bad child.

After a while, I gave in. The time in the hole broke me. I was eventually allowed to go back into the general population; I was broken to the point that I started helping pass out toothpaste and soap in the mornings, so I could be out of my cell. I got to know some of the other children who were locked up. Most of them were from East Palo Alto. We went to a co-ed school, and I ended up liking a boy that was in my class. He became my boyfriend even though there was no type of intimacy besides writing each other love notes. We even got to square dance with the boys on Wednesday nights. Square dancing was really corny, but we all participated and enjoyed ourselves. Square dancing was the only activity that the boys and girls were allowed to touch each other, so we made a time of it. I made sure that I behaved well, so I could participate and see my boyfriend.

If you acted up, you were not allowed to go to school or participate in square dancing. It is my guess that these "fringe benefits" were supposed to help us kids learn discipline, but it actually taught me how to become accustomed to being locked up and work as a slave. At first I was very bitter, but I learned how to "program," a term used by correctional staff that means you have the ability to adjust to the loss of freedom well. Now that I think about it, I don't believe learning how to cooperate with the policies and procedures that are imposed in a locked facility is a positive quality that children should acquire. Nevertheless, that was what I was expected to do.

The children I met in Juvenile Hall were a little older than I was and had a lot more street knowledge than I did. Most of them had been there before. I was only 14 years old at the time. Their conversations about life were well beyond my understanding, but I must admit I was fascinated. I listened to the juvenile vets with my nose wide open. Instead of being a place that helped me cope with my issues, Juvenile Hall became a criminal training facility for me. I didn't receive any counseling to help me deal with my issues, and the only things that I took away from that experience were negative.

Due to the pregnancy, I was assigned to different social workers, and I was confronted with the decision to keep or abort my baby. I chose to keep the baby. The focus of the sessions with the social workers revolved around the baby's life; not once was I asked about my life. My decision to keep the baby led me to be released from juvenile to an unwed mother's home in San Francisco. Nuns ran the program; it was a Catholic facility. My grandfather came to visit me at this facility, and he explained to me in so many words that he felt it wasn't wise to keep the baby. I was having second thoughts myself. When I expressed my second thoughts to the nuns at the program, I was immediately discharged and released to my grandparents. I later terminated the pregnancy.

That was the first time but not the last time that I would be locked up. When I first got locked up, I was very angry, and I had every right to be, but slowly but surely I became less and less angry and submitted to my feelings of powerlessness, which were provoked by my periods of incarceration. I basically gave up fighting the system and adjusted. I can see how my ability to function and not be so angry was looked upon as progress by the juvenile facility's staff, but I now realize that all I did was learn how to be in jail.

Chapter Two: The Effect

By the time I got out of juvenile hall on my first visit, I was not the same kid who went in. When I was returned to my grandparents, I was a very bitter, out of control child. I began to yearn for the lifestyle that I'd only heard about in juvenile hall, so I looked up some of the children I'd met. I got in touch with one girl who introduced me to a family that she was living with in East Palo Alto, and I ran away from my grandparents' home and began living in that house. The father in this family was not that fond of me and required sexual favors from me if I were to stay in his house.

I began thinking how could I get out of this situation, and I remembered the stories, or shall I say instructions, I'd heard in juvenile hall about burglarizing houses. I began to break into houses and steal clothes in order to take care of myself. (I was introduced to stealing when I was about nine years old while I lived at my father's house. As I mentioned previously, there was little food in his household, so sometimes my sister and I would go to the local supermarket and steal.)

I noticed that people treated me very differently when I had money in my pockets, and although I was only 15 years old, I gained respect in the streets. About three blocks from where I lived in East Palo Alto, there was a liquor store, Mickey's Liquor Store, where men and women stood and sold drugs 24/7, meaning every day of the week, holidays included. The parking lot was packed, and people listened to music, drank alcohol, smoked weed, and sold drugs all day and night. The store opened early in the morning and closed at 2 a.m. The crowd in front of this store was quite interesting: there were men who dropped off drugs to females who sold for them, a bunch of winos, a few men who sold their own drugs, a rare few women who sold drugs for themselves and a few youngsters who just hung out there.

I was intrigued by this lifestyle, and I ended up becoming friends with one of the women who sold weed on this corner. She was 19 years old at the time, and I was 15 although I told everyone that I was 17. This woman, whom I will refer to from here on out as Vett, had been recently released from jail. Vett kept her hair done nicely and wore cute clothes. Rumor had it that Vett could fight really well, and she had a big family who was well respected on the streets. I wanted to be like her. I watched her sell weed and picked up the trade. I became what was referred to back then as an "outlaw": a woman who sold drugs for herself rather than a man. I eventually became a good friend with Vett, and she also showed me how to steal clothes, which became one of my hustles.

Operating as an outlaw was very dangerous. People became jealous, particularly males who had women selling drugs for them, and on one occasion a man who was upset with my outlaw status took a bag of weed from me. Intending to shoot him, I left the liquor store to go retrieve a gun I had purchased earlier. By the grace of God, the gun didn't work properly, and the next day I was able to calm down because it was only a five dollar loss.

I really took to the wino crowd at the liquor store, especially Bugga and String Bean, both of whom I named. Bugga always had boogers in his nose, and String Bean wore a Del Monte T-shirt with a picture of a cartoon string bean on it that looked just like him because he was tall and skinny. I spent most of my time interacting with them while I sold my weed. They were very down to earth and kept me laughing. I love to laugh. I think they were also grateful that someone was willing to hold conversations with them. They just wanted some wine, and providing that for them made them loyal to me. For a mere couple of dollars, they watched out for the police and kept me entertained.

One thing I really liked about them is they weren't out to get me for much. I realize that they probably wouldn't have dealt with me if I had not provided them with alcohol, but that was only a couple of dollars. Everyone else I dealt with was out to get me for much more. Many people treated them differently because of the way they looked, but I didn't. I somehow was able to connect with their spirits, which were fun-loving. To this day, I still make connections with people that others deem to be hopeless.

Although I really admired Vett, one thing that didn't show that early on was that my newly found friend was a heroin addict. She shot heroin and sometimes cocaine on a daily basis. I used to go with her to get her dope, and sometimes I would go into the shooting gallery, a place where people gather to inject drugs, with her. She let me try snorting some of her heroin a few times, but I didn't like how heroin made me feel, how Vett's nose would run when she didn't have any heroin, how the other people in the gallery carried themselves, and I couldn't stand the sight of needles. However, I did like the high cocaine gave me, so I would pay $2 to go into the shooting gallery and snort cocaine.

I didn't know of anyone in the shooting gallery who was strung out on cocaine alone, so I thought it was an okay thing to do. I liked the way cocaine made me feel. I used to say that cocaine kept me "up on it," meaning I was aware of my surroundings. I thought it was different from being on heroin. At the time, cocaine was a very expensive drug, and I didn't do it every day at that point of my life. Back then, cocaine was referred to as "the white man's high", which meant it was too expensive for us.

Vett became more and more hooked on heroin and started to take advantage of my money and me. I started living with her, and she used me to watch her kids and pay most of her bills. At the age of 15, I decided to leave East Palo Alto and return to San Mateo County to live with my friend Jamie Lynn and her big sister. I'd known Jamie Lynn from the four years I spent living with my father. The event that caused the move resulted from a relationship I was having with Vett's younger brother, whom I let drive my car under the influence of Sherm, Sherman brand cigarettes dipped in embalming fluid; he turned all the way around to have a conversation with the people who were in the back seat and hit a tree.

I was in the passenger seat, and the bottom of my face was busted entirely open. I had to be rushed to the hospital for stitches. When I was released from the hospital, I went to San Mateo to look up some people who genuinely cared about me. Another reason I left was I was tired of supporting Vett's heroin habit. Vett's little brother was shortly afterwards convicted of serial rape and burglary, so I got out in the knick of time. I am told that Vett eventually died from AIDS.

When I was living with Jamie Lynn's family, I wasn't under as much financial pressure as I had been while living with a heroin addict, but I continued to sell weed. And at Jamie Lynn's house, I was allowed to see the proceeds because the household that I lived in genuinely loved me but could not afford to take care of me, so my illegal activities were accepted. In addition to selling weed, I also boosted clothes and worked for a living, and every now and then, I would enroll in some type of vocational course. I stayed busy and made a way for myself somehow despite I was only 15 years of age. I am amazed today at how much I accomplished on my own, especially when I am able to see how much my grown children are dependent upon me. I even managed to get a GED without the encouragement of parents and without being a part of a group who pursued education. Somehow I would always end up taking a course or two for something.

While I was living with Jamie Lynn, I participated in two talent shows at the Martin Luther King, Jr. Center with a couple of my closest friends. For the first talent show we danced to Zapp featuring Roger's song "Dance Floor." The next year we danced to Kurtis Blow's song "Tough." Each time we killed it! We practiced daily and had the best act two years in a row. These activities kept me focused despite the fact that I was selling drugs for a living. We practiced every single day, and my sister Latrice was our "manager." Even though I had to take care of myself at a young age, these activities allowed me to still be a child.

I loved and still love to dance; I will get the party started at random places, such as but not limited to the liquor store and the gas station. I failed to mention that I was elected as the best dancer in the 7th grade at Bowditch Middle School in Foster City. To this very day, I will dance at the drop of a hat. Music has kept me alive throughout my trials and tribulations. I will dance in the middle of the street without a partner. Therefore, I have many people in my life who love to see me drive up. A few of my children get a little embarrassed by my behavior, but I don't really care. Dancing makes me feel good, and I am able to let off a lot of steam.

When I was living in San Mateo, I was part of a group of about 15 teenagers that hung out together. I had some really good times in San Mateo. Although I was literally caring for myself at a very young age, I was able to make the best of it. I woke up every morning around 6 a.m. to sell my weed at the King Center. I was the only female out there. At the time, the local weed dealers had a mock union, which was called the Groundhog's Union. I took pride in being the only female member. However, many of the other dealers were on drugs, so they couldn't afford to buy the amount of weed I was buying. My sacks were much bigger than theirs because at the age of 15 I was buying pounds, and they were buying quarter ounces. They would get a little angry with me because I was getting all of the money. They had the audacity to ask me if we could take turns for the sales; I couldn't relate to the concept of holding on to illegal products while the next person gets some money. I firmly said no and told them if they wanted me to leave, they could buy me out, which they would commonly do.

I was making so much money that people were plotting to rob me. This one guy came home from the California Youth Authority, and I was told that he was planning to rob me. At the age of 16, I was a very dangerous girl, and I had to be in order to survive. After I received the news of the plotted robbery, I saw the guy, and I placed all of my money on top of the hood of my car and dared anybody to touch it, which was just plain stupid, but everyone ignored me, including the guy who was supposed to be robbing me.

This guy had just came home from the California Youth Authority and was known as the finest dude in town, and he was. This was back in the days when light skin and "good hair," a term used for hair that is not considered nappy, was the thing. The boys called him Kook and the girls called him Kookie. I began to like him and spoke about him to my friend Jamie Lynn. She told him, and we hooked up and had sex one night. The very next day he went back to jail for grand theft auto and was eventually sentenced to two years in state prison. He reached out to me from the jail and asked me to write him. I ended up waiting for him while he was in prison and sending him a gang of money while he was doing his two years from the proceeds of my weed sales.

When Kookie came home, I supplied his needs. I boosted clothes for him, and I gave him a great deal of money to survive on from my weed proceeds. A few of the teenagers in my crew were smoking cocaine, and he became interested. He got hooked for a period of time. That amounted to even more money that I was giving him. It was a good learning experience because I don't have a dime to give any man; I'd rather be alone with my money than broke with a man.

I used to have a lot of fun in my teenage years in San Mateo even though I was on my own at such a young age. I attended every concert, and I had a large group of friends. Even though I didn't have a driver's license, I kept a car and would transport my friends to the concerts. Most of the concerts were located at the Circle Star, an arena that had a rotating stage. I must be honest; we rarely paid to get into the Circle Star. We would run in the concert as a group. Whoever got caught, got caught. Fortunately, I never got caught.

I remember when Rick James came to the Circle Star. Back then, he was the man! He did three shows in a row. At the time, I was 7 months pregnant with my first child at the age of 19. Kookie, my baby's dad, didn't want me to go to the concert, but a good friend (who was also pregnant) and I did a Rayfield move (picked up clothes and ran out) on a maternity store, and I had clothes that were cute, so I went anyway. When we worked our way in, Rick James was walking down the center aisle, and we started screaming. I'll never forget that he looked at me as if I had shit on my face. He looked at me like "Bitch, please!"

I was trying to avoid seeing my baby's dad at the Rick James concert, but it just so happened that I was dancing and breaking it down to the ground at seven months pregnant off of the song "Super Freak" and my baby's dad walked up on me. Kookie looked extremely embarrassed. I didn't care, but later on when I got back to his mother's house, where I was living at that time, he asked me if I could please not go to the last show, and I didn't. I was tired from attending the previous two shows, so I wasn't mad.

It is funny because everybody who sold cocaine was trying to get enough to sell to Rick James, including my baby's dad. He said Rick had bought him out. My baby's dad came home in the wee hours of the morning on the last night of the concert trying to get in touch with people in East Palo Alto in order to get some cocaine for Rick James, who was staying at a local hotel. As I mentioned, I was seven months pregnant and very tired, so I didn't try to keep up.

Another thing about Kookie that made our relationship suffer was the fact that he was a player; he had women everywhere. We would fight a lot due to this fact, and his mother didn't like all of that fighting in her house, which I don't blame her. I wound up going back to San Francisco to my grandmother's house and eventually to an unwed mother's home. At the age of 19, I gave birth to Marvin, my first son, while I was living in the unwed mother's home. It took me three long days of agonizing back labor to have Marvin; I went in labor Friday the 13th and had him Monday the 16th. He was two weeks late, so he came out looking very wrinkled like an old man. Kookie and his cousins attended the birth and stayed for hours afterwards even when I went to sleep. I had no intentions of making Marvin a junior, but when I woke up everybody was gone, and there was a name written on the hospital bassinette the baby was in. It said "Marvin" in big bold letters, so I went along with it.

Kookie has since passed away from a car accident. Right before he passed, we became very good friends. He supported me in my academics and personal life. He was my first love, and we would have gotten married if it had not been for the invention of crack cocaine. I miss him dearly, and I WILL LOVE HIM ALWAYS. RIP, KOOKIE! The in-and-out-of-jail/prison cycle happened throughout our relationship, and Kookie was back in jail when I was pregnant with my second child, Kameshia. I was having a hard time living from post to post, and the pregnancy of my second child made it more difficult. I wound up living back with my grandparents for a few months, and I applied for public housing.

Chapter Three: The Invasion

In December 1984, at the age of 20, I moved into public housing, the Page Street Projects, located in the Western Addition of San Francisco, AKA the Fillmore, or better yet, Fillmoe. I was eight months pregnant with my second child. (My first child, Marvin, was 11 months old at the time.) When I first moved to the Page Street Projects, projects that were ironically painted in my favorite color pink, I can still remember watching folks from my back window walk around all day and night looking like they were under a spell in the parking lot. A lot of them were on heroin and have since died of AIDS, and a few others were seeking cocaine.

I was unfamiliar with seeing so many dope fiends at the same time. Project life was completely new to me. Although I had been involved in wrongdoing before, I had never seen wrongdoers in such numbers. They appeared to be very pitiful and hopeless, marching back and forth through the projects with no purpose in life. I believed that I was better than they were, and I can remember thinking to myself, "I will never be that damn stupid." It was an automatic assumption; however, by the time I figured out why these people were in such bad shape, I was one of them.

Another thing about the projects is it is a very, very close-knit community. A lot of people depend upon each other on many different levels in order to survive, so naturally I began to get to know some of the residents and people who hung out there. I guess I was seen as new fish, a term used for naïve newcomers, and although I had been in my share of trouble, I had not been exposed to this much game in my whole life, so I was extremely naïve. It hurts me now to think back and remember how much I was taken advantage of at such a young age, but such is life.

I gave birth to Kameshia in January of 1985, exactly two weeks after my first child's birthday. Kookie, was in prison at the time. Kameshia Aka Meeshia was very dark skinned at birth despite the fact that her dad was extremely light skinned. Although her facial features looked just like her dad, many people did not believe that Kookie was her father. When I pushed her out, I had to think back myself to try to figure out if the man I claimed was her dad was indeed her dad, but I hadn't had any sexual relationship with anybody but him, so he had to be the dad.

Meeshia was very sick at birth. She had a condition called Beta Strep, and she was in the intensive care unit (ICU) for about two weeks. I was told that she could be there for up to six months, but Meeshia had the will to live! Most children back in that era that had her condition didn't have the energy to eat, but Meeshia was named Miss Piggy by the nurses in ICU because she was extremely hungry. She was up and out of there expeditiously!

I went to see my sick baby every day while my first born was in daycare. When Meeshia was released from ICU, it was extremely hard trying to raise two children by myself at the age of 20 while their dad was in prison. The day I brought Meeshia home, Marvin didn't pay much attention to her, but when I turned out the lights and he figured out that she was staying he began to scream and cry. Marvin's crying woke Meeshia up, and she started to cry; then I started to cry.

The fact that Kookie's family, who were light skinned Creoles, didn't want to accept the fact that one of their family members produced a black baby didn't help matters. The weird part is that Greatgrandma, the brightest skin colored family member and matriarch of the family, looked at Kameshia when she saw her and said, "Look at her. Cuttin ' them eyes just like Kookie." She knew her family on sight, but the rest of the family refused to help me with her or even acknowledge her as being a family member. Instead, they wanted to interact just with my firstborn. That took a toll on me. However, later on, DNA testing proved that Kookie's high yellow ass produced a beautiful chocolate baby girl.

The same year Meeshia was born, on Father's Day, June 1985, my grandfather, Pa Pa, passed away. I was supposed to go see Pa Pa in the hospital that day, but I decided that since my kids' father was in the penitentiary, I was technically a father, so I did a little celebrating myself, figuring I would go see Pa Pa the morning after Father's Day, which was a day too late. I carried and still carry—I realize as I am typing these words—a lot of guilt around that. I missed the opportunity to see him for the last time, and he meant the world to me.

It is important that I talk about the relationship that I had with my grandfather because the loss of this relationship played a part in a life changing experience, drug addiction. When I was a child, my grandfather and

I would be home alone, and we would blast the music from my grandfather's stereo really loud and dance until we were both sweating. My grandfather would even hit the half splits sometimes. (The half splits are done by hitting the ground and keeping one leg outstretched while the other is bent.) If my grandmother, Mai Mai, would come home and catch us, she would fuss. We wouldn't complain because we knew the music was very loud. I LOVED to dance with my grandfather.

My grandfather was a diabetic and had to inject insulin every day, and although he would be considered sickly by some folks, he was the coolest man in the whole wide world to me. He was so cool he walked with an ornamented cane that he didn't need for disability purposes. Pa Pa was a handsome, dark skinned man, and since he was a barber, he kept up his facial hair, a goatee and moustache, immaculately. Not to mention, everybody knows that all types of goods come through Black barbershops, so the man stayed dressed clean. Sometimes he would wear a beret when he was feeling his New Orleans roots. My man was a "sharp cat" (he used phrases like that all the time), and I adored him.

During the exact same time period that Meeshia was born and Pa Pa died (1985), as if to music (I'm saying as if to music because music, at least the music that I like to listen to, has a timing and a beat, that I naturally follow), my community was strategically bombarded with a new, cheap, highly addictive form of cocaine, CRACK, and a new dope fiend was born, the CRACKHEAD. That's when ALL HELL BROKE LOOSE!! When this new drug hit the scene, I was unaware of its consequences, unlike I was aware of the consequences

34

of using heroin, because I had no examples to go by. All the people who used crack in this time period were human guinea pigs because it was new.

Despite my father's abusive treatment, I stayed in touch with him throughout the years. Right around the time my grandfather died, my father must have been aware of the new money making potential of cocaine because he told me that he had a friend who sold powder cocaine, and he asked me if I wanted to make some money. Powder cocaine wasn't as popular after crack hit the scene, but it was just a matter of cooking it up to make it lethal. During this time period, I didn't know how to cook crack (then referred to as "ready rock"), so I looked for someone in the projects who could.

There was only one crackhouse in the projects during the beginning of the crack epidemic, and it was called the Blue Door. (The front door of the unit was painted blue, and all of the other units' front doors in the projects were painted brown.) I don't remember asking them to cook the crack or when I took my first hit of crack cocaine, but I do sort of remember dealing with them because they were the only ones I knew who had a crack pipe or were able to cook crack. (Somehow many important facts have been conveniently erased from my memory bank; perhaps, my brain has chosen to erase certain painful memories as a defense mechanism to remain sane.)

Even though I was previously known as a go-getter and managed to make a way for myself in many different situations from an early age, I was no match for this deadly recipe of cocaine cooked down with baking soda and water combined with my desire to numb the pain from my grandfather's death. The number of crackheads seemed to multiply by the day, and I was one of the newest recruits. I didn't realize what was happening to me until it was too late; I had then become what is known today as a full-fledged CRACKHEAD.

Many people are offended by the word crackhead and want to define themselves or others by something else. This is the word I have chosen to identify myself with. I don't want to sugarcoat my ugliness, and I am downright UGLY when I am on this drug. I have spent almost most of my adult life in an aggressive, point blank, and straight-to-the-point environment, public housing. I am not used to downplaying what is foul or ugly, and I won't make an attempt to do that here. I believe it only prolongs the length of time that I allow myself to be that way.

I am not a person to make light of what crack cocaine has done to me or what I will do under its influence. When I was under the influence of this drug, it was all that was allowed to be on my mind. Crack cocaine has the ability to make me forget everything that matters, and because the need to keep getting high is so intense, it outweighs all. Fresh air or a clean glass of water, despite the fact that I may not have had either for days at a time, didn't outweigh my need to smoke crack. Therefore, I choose not to water down who I am, or shall I say WHAT I am, while under its spell, which is a CRACKHEAD.

Chapter Four: Year One
AKA The Year of the Rock

There is a moment of time that I am unable to account for, which is the point that I got hooked. My transformation into another being didn't take place after my first hit of crack; however, I don't know when it took place. I know that it happened in the time period between my grandfather's death and the day the woman suggested that I look in the mirror. Obviously, I lost time somewhere within my first year of addiction. Who knows? I may have been hooked by the first hit that I took, but I do know for a fact that that hit didn't have the same outcome as the many to follow. I wish I could identify the point that my brain became a one-tracked, crack-focused muscle, but I really and truly cannot. Perhaps the ability to conceal when it takes over is one of the many tricks of crack addiction.

The first year of my crack addiction at the mere age of 20 years old was the roughest. I would accept damn near anything, any type of treatment, and I did damn near everything to get drugs. I began to let any and everyone into my house to get high regardless to the fact that there were two young children in my household. One particular night I let someone in who was a dope shooter but had a few dollars to give me for letting him shoot dope in my bathroom. God rest his soul; he has since died from Hepatitis C, but I did let him know that he had an important role in my autobiography before he left this earth.

The cocaine that he shot in my bathroom made him super paranoid to the point that he held my friend and me at knifepoint when he came out of the bathroom. The look in his eyes was DEADLY scary, and he also had the reputation of being a cold and calculated killer. My friend, whom I will refer to as Lady Kay, one of the few people in the drug world that I will call a friend in this book, was an older woman in her 50's who had just got turned out to crack cocaine. She was about 30 years older than me at the time. She was one of the people that I had previously thought was stupid for wandering endlessly in the projects as if she were extremely tired and her feet hurt.

According to what Lady Kay told me, she had worked most of the earlier years of her adult life as a social worker in New York. I call her a friend because we were able to laugh and talk together. She was a cold dope fiend and so was I, but I loved her, and she loved me. She was very stingy with her dope though, and I had to cut her socks with a razor one day while she was asleep in the wee hours of the morning to take some of the crack that she claimed she didn't have.

She woke up in a stupor clapping her hands and crying because the dope was gone out of her socks, and she was supposed to be selling it for someone else. I didn't know that it was someone else's dope. All I knew is that whenever she lit her crack pipe it sounded as if she were frying chicken. The crack she allotted me made minimal noise because it was so little. After she gave me these microscopic hits of crack that did nothing but tease my addiction, she had the audacity to go to sleep with a sock full of crack. I felt bad but not that bad. She lived in my house and ate my food for free. It was a cut throat environment.

She has since passed away; rest in peace, LADY KAY. Anyway to get back to the story, she had very large breasts, and the man that I let come in and shoot his dope thought that her breasts were some type of weapon and made her lift up her shirt so that he could see what was under there. When I got a chance, I ran out of my front door and down to my neighbor's house. My neighbor's brother was there, and he had a relationship with the guy I let in and was able to calm this guy down.

It was a very scary experience, and I told myself I would not let anybody back in my house again, but after a few days, I was back to letting people in to use my public housing unit as a drug station. My home had then become a full-fledged CRACKHOUSE. People gave me little or nothing 24 hours of the day or night to come in, and when my portion of crack they gave me was gone, I was required to compromise myself by doing all types of things for my company so that they would give me more.

I lived in constant humiliation. I had earned the new identity of a TOSS UP. A toss up is a person who sells his or her body for drugs. In the public housing setting, women are more openly used to provide these services; however, men do sexual favors for drugs as well in the closet. As I attempt to describe myself and ways of thinking when I earned this title, I am very saddened. My defense mechanism to block the memories wants to prevent me from exposing myself in this manner, but I think it is important that this vital part of feeding my addiction is discussed.

I HATED performing sexual acts for drugs. It was not something that I wanted to do; it was something I had to do. I believed I had no other options or resources, and therefore was willing to sell my soul for crack cocaine. The body was a sacrifice given in order to submit my soul. I couldn't remain present being the strong Black woman I was and sell parts of my body for chicken change. No, I had to give myself up totally to do so. Submitting my soul was the only way that I could survive committing such evil, heinous and illogical acts with any portion of my mind left afterwards. Otherwise, I would have gone nuts because what I did was so unlike ME. (I and ME were the struggling characters involved in my addiction. I was no longer one; I became divided due to the confusion and being required to follow through on acts that were beneath boundaries I was willing to stoop to, and thus ME, the selfish villain, gained more and more control.)

Ironically, the men who use the services of a toss up are not looked down upon as much as she is. However, she is more accepted today than she was back in those days, but she is still taken advantage of on a regular basis. Many of these toss ups have children and people who are emotionally attached to them, and many of the children who had to witness or still have to witness their mothers under this title are now the ones who are killing or being killed at a rapid rate. Although the toss up is perceived to have a low status in the community, her spiritual absence in the community has caused a wave of repercussions.

Not many memories of the early periods of my addiction are clear, but there is one particular day that has stuck with me. One day during the first year of my addiction, I was walking to Safeway with one of my "crack cousins," a term I used to describe people that I had regular crack dealings with. I cannot clearly remember what our motive was for walking there, but I do remember that we had run out of dope, so we must have had some scandalous scheme up our sleeves. This woman was the woman who helped me smoke up Christmas, meaning she assisted me with trading the presents I had for my children for crack. I was disgusted with her and with myself for being stupid enough to be with her.

As we were walking, I noticed that the woman I was walking with was tore up: she hadn't been to sleep in days, her hair was all over her head, she was very skinny, and her clothes were dirty. I was disappointed with myself and I thought, "This is the type of people I hang around with now." After looking her over, I looked myself over, and I was no better than she was. A part of me was forced to accept my new status as a dope fiend.

Eventually, my home was taken over during that first year, and I was in constant danger. My son was almost two years old and my daughter was almost one; I was 21. My children and I were captives in our own home. I sold my body for little or nothing on a regular basis to get more crack, and I got so bad I was unable to care for my two little babies anymore. I would leave them alone while I would go try to find more crack. The house was filthy, and there wasn't enough food available. Although there were a lot of people who came to my house, no one ever offered to help buy food. One day, a dealer was in my home with his entourage, and my two little babies and I were sitting up eating a plain loaf of bread. The dealer made a joke about us eating the plain bread and others laughed; I felt so low that I couldn't even defend myself anymore.

Chapter Five: How I Became
Reduced to a Fraction

I can remember one day I called Children Protective Services (CPS). I told them I had been using crack cocaine for about six months, and I needed help. Crack was still fairly new, and they were unaware of how bad off a person could be who had just been addicted six months, so they wrote me off, and I was unable to find a place that would take my family. Choices were very limited and still are for places that crack addicts can get help and keep the family intact. I wound up going to jail one day, and I had my kids with me at the time I was arrested. I was arrested for breaking into my then boyfriend's hotel room after finding out that he was living with another woman. I intended to take back some clothes I had stolen for him for Christmas. (That boyfriend is someone that I refuse to give an identity in my story lest it provide him with five undeserved minutes of fame.)

My former boyfriend was there when I was arrested, and after I was taken into custody, he turned my kids over to the police. Due to the previous phone call to CPS I made for help, I was not allowed to get my kids when I got out of jail. I was young at the time, but that is why I am now a firm believer in the right to remain silent. I do not speak with anyone of authority concerning my kids anymore because everything I say can and will be used against me in a court of law.

My children were returned to my home after a hearing about a month later, but I was still in bad shape. Eventually, they were removed from my household anyway. I can still remember my little daughter screaming as I put her in the car with the social worker. He had given me an ultimatum about cleaning up my house, which I did, but right before he was scheduled to visit, I went on another crack run, and the children trashed the place again. When he showed up on the agreed upon date and time, I handed over my children to him without a fight. One part of me was relieved because I really couldn't handle taking care of them, and my life seemed hopeless. But there was also another part of me that died when I handed my babies over, which was the part of me that was dignified. When the dignified part of me died, I was no longer a whole; I was reduced from a whole to a fraction.

I used to visit the children when my addiction allowed me to. I would sit and hold my kids and cry. I felt powerless. The kids were separated from each other, and they weren't doing well at all. They were very close being that they were one year and two weeks apart. My daughter Kameshia's hair was rarely combed when I saw her, and she was very withdrawn, but she loved for me to hold her. On one visit, I noticed that she had welts that, judging from my experience, I believed had been made with a belt. I told the social worker this, but she didn't take me seriously. That's another one of the repercussions that come with being a crackhead; your opinions and thoughts are not respected nor taken seriously. My son, Marvin, was not doing well either. When he was two years old, they sent him to a children's mental facility in Napa because he was doing himself bodily harm. He would bang his head and scratch his face up. I was cracked out at the time, and I didn't know how to handle all of this news sober.

Instead of using the loss of my children as an inspiration to get clean, I sank deeper into my addiction. I was very ashamed of myself, and my negative self-talk was worse than ever before. I no longer had a reason to thrive. I merely survived. How can one learn to love and make a comeback when she has participated in such hateful decisions that affected her babies? I would stay high to be able to live with myself. I thought if I were to be present I would lose my mind because of all of the dirt I had done.

I hated the CPS workers, and I couldn't bring myself to act as if I didn't. My hostility led them to believe that I was crazy just like they felt my two-year-old was. I was diagnosed as needing psychiatric care, a diagnosis that commonly takes place if someone cannot submit to authority or adapt well to extreme losses. One social worker, an uptight Chinese woman (I WILL NEVER FORGET HER NAME, BUT I'M GOING TO GIVE HER A PASS), thought that it would be best if my first two kids didn't know their parents at all and refused to let the paternal grandmother remove the kids from foster care. I was on crack, and Kookie was in prison at the time, so the CPS worker felt my babies would be better off not ever knowing their parents despite the fact an able family member was willing to take them.

Excuse my language, but that CPS bitch couldn't have cared less about my babies. She was more concerned with making sure that they didn't EVER get to know their parents. She never considered them being able to know their family. In her eyes, Kookie and I were the worst parents, and even though she didn't have anywhere solid for the kids to go and they were separated, she refused to release them to family. She was wrong, over-the-top, and had no idea what she was doing. The system did not love my children, but she saw fit for them to stay in the system. I hated that woman with a passion, and she damn near drove me crazy.

Eventually, the paternal grandmother couldn't cope with the uptight, Asian CPS worker's tactics combined with the pressure that her only son applied on her to get his kids out of the system, so she ended up slapping the CPS worker in the face during a visit. Everyone was worried about what the outcome would be because of the assault, but things worked out for the best. Another social worker, a Black man, was assigned to the case, and he released the children (who had been held hostage for close to four years by this time) to their paternal grandmother in a few weeks time after he was assigned to their cases. It is unfortunate that physical violence had to be used before my children were released, but sometimes you have to take extreme tactics for extreme people.

Chapter Six: Adjusting to My New Status

My crack addiction was very tricky. It had the capability to replace all of my loved ones with people who couldn't care less about my well-being and would constantly disappoint me, lie to me, try to take advantage of me, and prey upon me. Nevertheless, that is the crowd I surrounded myself with while I was on crack cocaine; the people could be more toxic than the crack at times. Although I grew to hate some of the people in my crack network system, I still kept them near because in all actuality I was one of them. There are a vast array of emotions and self-brainwashing that one must go through in a 24 hour period just to deal with the irrational behaviors and consequences of this type of lifestyle.

I would like to take a moment to try to explain exactly what my crack addiction is like. The need for this drug surpasses the need for air, water or food. While under the influence of this drug, I am no longer able to focus on anything else. It doesn't matter what I had to look forward to or had going for myself, somehow crack minimized all of my blessings, assets and strengths, causing me to throw all that really mattered away. This is not only a mind-controlling drug, but it is also a drug that aggressively takes hostage and effectively controls the spirit as well. Just imagine that you couldn't fully control or trust your own thinking, and you will have some insight into what crack addicts go through on a regular basis even when they have managed to clean themselves up. As soon as the smoke was blown out, it seemed as if a mind-manipulating, irrational, incapable of loving, no-conscience having, suicidal and homicidal beast took over my entire body.

It took time to learn how to live past the desperation that accompanied my addiction. I had to learn to manage what I would and wouldn't do for crack. I found that the more desperate I was to get high, the less likely I was to get some drugs. I can truly relate to the slogan, "Never let 'em see you sweat." Some activities such as exchanging sex for drugs and allowing people to take advantage of me just didn't rest right even when I was under the influence. Thus, the naïve period of my addiction came to an abrupt end around the second year. I learned how to do other things besides sell my body.

One of the skills that I picked up was the ability to cook dope. Local dealers would come to my house, and I would cook up their dope for them. The majority of the dealers who would come were teenagers. Back then, there was a lot of money being made off crack, and the pay was extremely good. I got really attached to one of the teenagers who chose to make a living from selling crack. He was 15 years old, and at the time, I was around 22 years old. He was very special to me because despite my status as a crackhead, he confided in me with his problems. He listened to my advice and respected my mind. He didn't know it, but he helped me a great deal. When you are a crackhead, people do not take you seriously, but this one child respected my mind despite my faults.

Most of his problems were based upon his hustling capabilities. He was wondering why he could not "come up" (a term used to describe making money) despite the fact that he put in work every day. I acted as his advisor and let him know that his entourage was too large and he needed to shake them if he wanted to see any proceeds. He traveled with a group of about six or seven boys, and he kept them all high. It may seem as if I gave a child ill advice, and I was a grown woman, but I was just a baby in the game myself. I told him what I thought was right. I knew what I had to do to make money back in the day, so I told him the same: shake loose from your friends. My new teenaged friend took my advice, and every day he came with a larger amount of cocaine for me to cook. He started with a sixteenth of an ounce and worked his way to a quarter pound. This enabled me to stop selling my body. I also pulled my old clothes boosting skills out of the closet, so I began to dress myself a little better and had a supplemental income when I was not cooking up dope. I was no longer a tossup.

During the first year of my addiction, I was physically abused a great bit. I was beaten, raped and verbally abused. For some reason the crack made me afraid to fight back, but during the second year I began to become more aggressive; I had to. I was very feisty prior to getting on dope, and I began to use some of the fighting skills that I had acquired during my teenage years. I am a very little person, and in addition, I was on crack, so I became a target for many grown ass bullies.

There was one young lady who picked on me on a regular basis. I normally wouldn't fight back, but my newfound teenaged friend was not having it. The young lady wanted to fight me for no reason, and my teenaged friend told me, "Marl, you better fight back." When the fight began, the young woman started wailing on me, but my little friend kept saying, "You better fight back." Although this woman got me on the ground and was beating me in my face, I somehow summoned the strength to get her off of me and started winning the fight. I earned the respect of my peers, and finally I wasn't subjected to any more bullying. During this time period, I very rarely lost a fight, and I began to get more respect. I earned the name "Big Marl," which is ironic because I am only four feet eleven inches tall.

On another occasion, I was cooking up a great deal of dope for my teenaged friend and his buddies. While I was cooking up the dope, a woman that I used to get high with started making a whole bunch of noise, and I was scared to death because of the amount of dope that was in my house. During this time period, we didn't only have to worry about the real police, but we also had to worry about the Housing Authority police, which was compiled of a group of extremely crooked individuals. On one occasion, the Housing Authority police entered my crackhouse and took a quarter ounce of dope without taking anyone to jail. Years later, I recognized the Housing Authority police officer who did that in a crackhouse, and now I know what his angle was back then.

When I asked my noisy friend to please keep her voice down, she kept rambling irrelevant facts and showing off in front of the youngsters in my unit. (God knows I wish I had been born a bigger person, so I wouldn't have been picked on as much.) I ended up socking her in the eye with ALL OF MY MIGHT. Her eye swelled up as if she had been in a professional boxing match. She wound up leaving, but when I did see her again, she let me know that she had to have surgery on her eye. She said her doctor asked her for the name of the man who had done that to her, and she responded, "His name is Marilyn." I didn't like that I did that, but I did what I had to do, so it wouldn't be done to me.

I figured out that I had to turn into someone else in order to be respected and survive, so I became a cold, heartless, predatory creature. By this time, I had adapted to my environment. I was a vital part of the drug-motivated economy that was the center of the public housing site I lived in. I knew every addict, every dealer, every line that could be used to try to trick me, every line that could be used to trick others, every spot to smoke dope in, etc. My entire life revolved around crack cocaine. I doubt if I left a six-block radius within a two-year time span. There was no need to. Everything I NEEDED could be supplied within this minimal radius.

Another thing that needs to be also noted is that people from all areas come to the projects for drugs, so my crack network system was larger than one would probably imagine. Project life worked hand and hand with my addiction. Who could ask to be addicted in a better place? The drugs were plentiful, people came from miles around to get drugs from this location, and it was accepted as a viable income.

I eventually abandoned the public housing unit in the Page Streets Projects and lived from pillar to post for the next several years. It became overwhelming to live in that environment with my addiction. I didn't want to be like I was, but I didn't know what to do about it. I constantly prayed and cried for help, but I was in a situation that was beyond my control. What was happening to me was bigger than me, so I left the Page Street Projects because I couldn't handle living there.

Chapter Seven: Ellesse

In the third year of my addiction I became pregnant with my third child, and I used crack cocaine throughout the entire pregnancy. The guy I was pregnant by managed to take better care of himself than I did (although he was on dope too), and he was ashamed that I was claiming he was the father of my child. He denied the possibility of this being his child. To be honest, it was either him or a trick, but something told me it was him, and later DNA testing proved me right.

I went in labor in the crack house. I can remember how it went down. I was living in a hotel provided by the welfare office for homeless pregnant women and women with children. This hotel was located in the Mission District on Valencia Street right across from the Valencia Gardens Housing Project. It was filthy. All of the carpet needed to be removed, the walls were super dirty, and there was a weird odor throughout the entire building. If you've ever been around addicts whose hygiene is not up to par, you know the odor I'm talking about. There were so many dope fiends in the building I could literally smell the dope coming out of their pores. Not to mention I was nine months pregnant, and there's something about pregnancy that makes my sense of smell keener. The hotel was downright disgusting. People ran in and out of the building all hours of the night. I had just applied for aid and had not received a check, so I managed to get around five days clean when I first moved in.

Shortly thereafter, a check arrived for 500-some-odd dollars, and the chase was on. I went on a severe run in the Page Street Projects and ended up going into labor at a crackhouse. They could only convince me to let them call the ambulance by promising me a hit of crack. I didn't want to deal with the reality of having a baby, but I was out of money, so there wasn't much I could do. I never got the hit, and the ambulance arrived. When the ambulance arrived, I was so paranoid that I jumped up from the gurney while en route to see if the police were following us. My conscience was getting to me. I knew I was wrong, and it was time to answer. This was 1987. Crack babies were a huge topic back then, and I was about to deliver one, so that made me a crack mother. A crack mother received no mercy; she was the lowest of the low.

When I arrived at the hospital, I asked for some cranberry juice. I had heard that cranberry juice would help flush drugs out of your system. I don't know if I was high or if this is true, but I could have sworn the juice they gave me was very watered down. I thought they were watering it down to make sure it didn't change the drug test results. I asked the doctor if there was any way he could stop the labor. He said I was only three weeks premature, and he wasn't going to try to stop it. Up until that point, I was very angry and had been treating the staff at the hospital mean, but nature set in and I had to submit. When we got to the labor room and it was time to push, I stopped pushing and made a confession at the top of my voice: "I have been smoking crack and haven't been to sleep in five days. If there's anything wrong with the baby, I did it!"

I pushed her out, and there she was: the prettiest newborn baby I had ever seen in my life. Her head was perfectly shaped. My baby, a beautiful, curly headed, brown-skinned, perfect-faced baby girl, was placed on a CPS hold and taken at birth. She stayed at the hospital for about a week. I secretly slept in empty rooms at the hospital and visited her every day and night. I guess the nurses in the nursery were aware of the CPS hold on my baby and my status as a crack mother because they were very rude and dry. One nurse told me my baby was asleep when I showed up. I politely ignored the nurse and removed my baby from the little baby bed they had her in and held her. I knew I wasn't going to be able to hold her much when she left the hospital, so I went up there day and night. I also knew that I wasn't going to know where she was after she left the hospital. I had two kids who were already in foster care, and I didn't know where they were.

The separation from my baby was devastating. I grieved all of the time. One moment we were one. The next moment all I had was a battered body due to the birth and no baby. I was a mess psychologically. This loss would stay with me, and I randomly had breakdowns throughout the years to come. I had one more reason to get high.

Many people are very judgmental of women who are addicted to drugs and still have children. I cannot speak up for myself in a way to justify such behavior, but I will attempt to explain. Birth control and protection require the ability for one to have some type of respect for her body. I didn't care. I don't mean I didn't care about having a baby. I just didn't care. I couldn't envision myself as having a body. My body didn't matter. Consequences were not something that I was able to fathom. I didn't seek prenatal care, and therefore I didn't get any positive reinforcement about the pregnancy. At first I concealed the pregnancy, but she grew bigger and bigger.

To be brutally honest, the need and urge for crack during my pregnancy was much, much stronger than when I wasn't pregnant. I was two addicts in one. However, deep down inside I didn't want to harm my baby. You see, deep down inside a lot of things were happening that weren't allowed to surface. The crack didn't allow me to petition on my baby's behalf; it was not a democracy. I was a war prisoner under strict dictatorship. Who can think of a more brilliant way to hold someone captive than within her own skin? Think about it; where can she go?

During this time period, I used my grandmother as a crutch to get more drugs. At first she didn't know what I was doing, but I finally told her. She supported my habit for years. When she didn't want to, I would act a fool, and she wound up getting a well-deserved restraining order against me that would eventually lead me to prison. Once when I went to visit my daughter Ellesse at the place provided by Children Protective Services, I snuck out of the back door with her. I went to my grandmother's house for money, and she called the police. I was sentenced to six months in the county jail for kidnapping. Upon release, I continued to smoke crack, and I became a habitual consumer of the criminal justice system.

Chapter Eight: Harriet Tubman

Two years later, while in a drug program in East Palo Alto, I gave birth to my fourth child, a son. When I was about seven months pregnant, I arrived at my grandmother's door and asked her to call the police. I was on probation, and I hadn't been to see the probation officer. I can remember walking around and talking to myself; I had been up for four or five days, and I was truly out of my mind. The only thing that I could think of for help was jail, so I went to my grandmother's house and asked her to call the police. I was taken to jail and received a drug program as my sentence. I wasn't picked up from jail by the program until my 9th month pregnant.

The program I went to was for women with children, and it was called Harriet Tubman. It was located in an apartment building in East Palo Alto across the street from the gambling shack. I was assigned to a counselor named Fred. Every week I would have to go to sessions with Fred. I then realized how much crack cocaine had ruined my self-esteem. Although I had been clean for a few months counting the county jail time, I was still unable to look in the mirror. That was what Fred wanted me to do, and I wasn't about to tell myself, "I love you," as instructed.

Those sessions were very painful. I disclosed to Fred that I was a toss-up and was very ashamed. One day while we were in group session, Fred told the rest of the group, "Marilyn sells her body for crack." I jumped up and ran out of the room. I hated Fred and wouldn't speak to anybody in the program for about three days. I couldn't believe that he put my business out there like that. After my third day of silence, something happened on the inside. I began to feel relieved because what I perceived to be my worst secret was out. Ironically, other women began to admit their shortcomings in group. One woman admitted to "pawning" her daughter for a 20-shot of crack, and another woman admitted to giving oral sex to a dog. I hadn't gone that far, and I am not saying that to portray myself as better than these women. I'm saying that because I realized that I could do worse. I guess Fred knew what he was doing when he put me out there.

I managed to complete the program, and because I had been sentenced by the court, I had to leave as soon as my six months were up. I went to live with a woman who was a counselor at Harriet Tubman and her kids. Living with her didn't work out because she was extremely bossy and grouchy, so my son and I returned to San Francisco and lived in a hotel under the homeless program for about three weeks. I once again applied for the public housing waiting list under the "as is" program. Public housing units under the "as is" program had all types of problems. My unit didn't even have a front door when I signed the lease.

The "as is" program was found to be illegal and was discontinued. However, before it was eliminated, I was able to get another public housing unit in the Sunnydale Housing Project in about a three-week time span. I managed to stay crack free for a couple of years and regained custody of my oldest daughter, but their grandmother would not give me my oldest son back. I did well for a period of time; however, my younger son's father came home from prison and was very abusive, and I was living in a drug infested environment, the projects. After 2 ½ years clean, I ended up relapsing, and my children's relatives had to take over for me once again.

Chapter Nine: Back and Forth/In and Out

Throughout my addiction, I sampled many different drug programs. Sometimes I would go to detox when I was tired. I've had some memorable moments in some of these places. For example, back in the early 1990's I went to a detoxification program for men and women at the Salvation Army. I liked this place because you didn't have any chores and were allowed to eat, drink and sleep your way back to health. However, we were not allowed to do certain things. One of the rules was that no food could be brought in from the outside. One day, a country white man from Texas, whom we called Tex, was getting a pass to San Francisco General Hospital, but his real reason for leaving was because he was expecting an SSI check that he wanted to go pick up.

We, meaning a couple of the other detox patients and I, convinced Tex to pick up some Kentucky Fried Chicken on the way back. When he got back, he was so high he couldn't even stand up straight. We got just enough information from him to find out that someone was outside, just behind the building, holding two buckets of chicken. The other two patients went outside and persuaded the guy holding the buckets to "throw the chicken over!" The man who had the buckets in his possession claimed not to speak good English, but through words and gestures he finally understood what they were saying.

It was mid afternoon, and we all decided to skip dinner and eat our chicken later on that night when the cool staff got on duty. At around 11 p.m., we all woke up to go eat the chicken. When the bucket was opened, the only contents it contained were biscuits. We were all hungry and disappointed until one of the men said, "Now, if that would have been some dope, we would have checked it by now," and we all fell out laughing.

A few days later, I got a pass to go home to the Sunnydale Housing Project to get some clothes, and I discovered that everything I owned had been stolen while I was in detox. All of the things—I mean every last thing—that I accumulated over the couple of years I had been clean had disappeared with a blink of an eye. I was outdone. Although prior to seeing my empty house I had gained new friends and developed a plan to "make it," I left the detox without thinking twice. The loss was tremendous, and I wasn't accustomed to feeling. I never returned to that public housing unit.

I guess I would be considered homeless during periods of time, but I never did sleep on the streets, nor have I ever waited in a food line. My remedy for homelessness was staying awake and incarceration. I rarely ate, and when I was hungry I would steal food from local grocery stores. Although I never slept on the sidewalk or in a doorway, one night I did sleep in an abandoned car, which was an ugly experience in the morning. The mornings were a very crucial and depressing time for me. Normally, I am a morning person, but for a person who was waking up to nothing, the brightness that only early morning has to offer tended to highlight my filthiness, especially if there wasn't any money in my pockets, which tended to be the trend.

Although I didn't physically have a reliance on crack (I had no aches and pains if I didn't get it), the mental games and urges were practically unbearable. Waking up without or running out of dope would make the brightness come out and examine my entire being even if it was pitch dark outside. The brightness represented reality, and reality is not a good place when all is hopeless.

Chapter Ten: Prison

I was back and forth from the streets to programs to incarceration. Finally, I wound up in state prison at the age of 27. I can remember feeling sad when the bus arrived at the county jail about 3 a.m. to pick us up for the prison ride. When I got to Chowchilla, I was taken to a place called R & R, which stands for Receiving and Release. A bunch of other women were sitting around talking and waiting to hit the yard. The first yard I went to was for newly arrived prisoners, A Yard. While on this yard, prisoners were evaluated for health and psychological purposes before they went to their final prison or prison camp destinations. We were only allowed to come outside two hours per day on this yard.

During my stay on A Yard, I became sick as a dog, so I put in a slip to be seen by a doctor. The sickness lasted about three weeks, and that request to be seen has not been answered to this very day. I remember desperately wanting to get out of the "new arrival" status and get to where I was going. I began to look forward to going to another prison because I would have more privileges and a better chance to live if I got sick because I could have more access to the free world. No phone calls were allowed while we were on this status, and the turnaround time for mail was about a month.

I hated A Yard. The correctional officers were always screaming and hollering at us. That's what they do when you first arrive. I don't know if all of that hollering was supposed to break me down, but it made me nervous. One day we were walking to the chow hall for breakfast, and we were not supposed to talk to each other because that is the rule. It had been raining, and there were puddles of mud all over the yard. I accidentally stepped in the mud, and it felt like quicksand because the mud went well above my ankles. We laughed, and we weren't supposed to. This mean ass correctional officer who loved to yell came over and screamed at me to "shut up" at the top of his voice. He didn't know it, but I got teary eyed. Later on that morning after breakfast we were cleaning the unit, and I went to find that officer. I quietly told him I was an abused child and asked him to please not yell at me like that ever again. He said, "Okay," and never yelled at me again.

Another reason I hated A Yard is because women were in and out of the dorms going to different facilities, so you really couldn't get attached to anybody. There were six beds in each room, and generally it was diverse, meaning there were two blacks, two whites and two Hispanics. One night a bus arrived, and I got three new cellmates. I'm not sure where they came from, but they stayed up all night laughing and talking. They did this for two nights straight. I was extremely tired and uncomfortable. After we got back from breakfast, a Hispanic lady that was at least 10 years my elder said, "Okay, it's time to make noise." I told her I was tired and she was making me uncomfortable. She responded, "This ain't a mothafuckin' convalescent home; this is the mothafuckin' penitentiary!" Then she rattled off her prison number, which was an old number, and she told me I was a new commitment. (A new commitment is someone who just got to prison with a new conviction). She spoke about the fact that she had been coming to the penitentiary for years as if it were an accomplishment. She then made the mistake of calling me a "punk ass bitch."

This was my first time going to prison. All I knew about prison was what I saw on television. I sincerely believed if I didn't act there was no telling what this woman would do to me. I got off my bunk and started beating the shit out of her like my life depended on it. We fought one round, and they broke it up, but she kept talking, so we started again only this time she kept trying to get to her locker. I didn't know what she was trying to get to in her locker. That scared me to death, and I really started to go to work on her. I pulled her out from the corner where her locker was by her hair and kept beating her in her face. She still wanted to fight. I beat her for a third round, and that's when my cellmate, a black woman from Redding, screamed, "You are going to lose your date!" She was referring to my date to be released. That brought me back to reality, so I stopped.

The Hispanic woman was still talking mess, but I didn't say anything. However, everybody slept well that night, and she was quiet as a mouse. Come to find out, she had brought in some powder cocaine, and they were all high. That's why they couldn't sleep, and that's why she was so cocky. I grew to have respect for her because she was pretty beat up, but she didn't tell on me. She was unable to go to chow hall because of her injuries, so food had to be stolen from chow hall and brought to her. I even brought her some food. We grew to be on speaking terms over the years that we passed each other's paths in correctional facilities.

After a couple of months on A Yard, I finally went before the committee, so I could be transferred from the receiving yard to another prison, and I was sent to Northern California Women's Facility, AKA Stockton. This prison held approximately 700 women and was very quiet and boring. I was super disappointed when I got there because I was led to believe it I was going to have a good time, but instead you could hear a pin drop on the yard. When we were on the A Yard at Chowchilla, we could hear the boom boxes playing music on the other yards; this was not the case in Stockton. This was a very quiet, controlled setting. I was told by some of the prisoners that Stockton was where a lot of baby killers and snitches were sent, and that's why it was so controlled.

After I got to Stockton, I still had to go to a unit that had minimal yard time, the same two hours per day. I had to wait to find out what job I would be assigned to in order to get full privileges. After a few weeks, I found out what type of job I was to receive in order to earn "good time work time." Good time work time means a prisoner that works gets two days credit towards their sentence for every day spent in prison. Up until that point, I was on third time, meaning I got three days credit towards my sentence for every two days served. Basically, having a prison job cuts the sentence in half.

All of the prisoners in Stockton went before a panel of individuals that decide what type of prison job would be suitable for a particular prisoner. When I got pregnant with my second child years prior to this, I completed a legal secretarial program, and I learned how to type pretty fast. In order to brush up on my clerical skills, I requested to be allowed to work in Key Data, which was a clerical prison job that supported the Department of Motor Vehicles. Nevertheless, it was deemed that I needed to work in the prison laundry. I couldn't understand why they found it better for me, a person with pretty good clerical skills, to wash clothes than brush-up on my skills and possibly become more employable upon release.

When I got to my assignment, I found out that I had to work on the soiled side. We received laundry from Agnew Mental Hospital and a couple of other correctional facilities. The laundry that we received from the mental hospital was the worst. We had to sort the laundry while it was going down a single conveyor belt. The shitty and pissy laundry was okay to be sorted and go straight down the conveyor belt; however, we had to push the laundry that had blood and hair on it to the back of the conveyor belt and another female prisoner who wore protective clothing put the items in a bin that was double washed.

The workers at the mental hospital obviously knew the laundry was coming to prisoners because they sent it to us with used IVs, colostomy bags, big pieces of shit and other gross things that could have simply been discarded; instead, these gross items were wrapped inside of the sheets and clothes. Lint from this filthy environment was constantly in our noses and mouths. One of the worst parts of job was we worked in stifling heat, and even though we were provided with masks, we rarely used them because they made it harder for us to breathe.

When I saw this stuff coming down the conveyor belt for the first time, I fell to my knees and openly asked God, "Why did you leave me here like this?" A voice in my mind replied, "It was you who left me." That was the very first time I believe I actually heard from God. While I was crying and praying out loud, the other women were bent over laughing really hard and saying that my behavior was typical for everyone's first day on the job. To top it off, lunchtime fell in the middle of our shift, and we had to leave this mess and go eat.

After a while, I got used to the job and began to appreciate the little $42 per month I earned because I didn't have much money coming from anywhere else. I learned to start having fun with the other women while on duty by telling jokes, singing and doing whatever else was possible to keep my mind off what I was required to do if I wanted to go home as scheduled. That was my first but not last prison sentence. It became easier and easier to go back. My first prison sentence is the most memorable.

During my first prison sentence, there was a correctional officer who didn't seem to be very happy with herself. She was a very bitter, slimly built young Black woman, perhaps in her late 20's. She was kind of on the homely side. All of the other Black correctional officers and even prisoners kept their hair immaculate; hair is an important factor in the women's prison. We had nothing but time, and a lot of time was spent looking pretty. Even the female correctional officers made sure their hair was done nicely. It was kind of like a competition. Keeping our hair done was an extremely big deal. During the week, I kept my hair wrapped up in a scarf because I worked in the laundry, but on the weekends many of the other women and I went out of our way to make sure our hair was pretty for yard time. However, this particular correctional officer wore her hair in a little tiny, brushed-back, permed ponytail daily. She also wore cheap work shoes in comparison to her co-workers. There were rumors that circulated in the prison that she was on dope. This officer would work hard to provoke an inappropriate response from the prisoners; she seemed to be jealous of us, which is ironic.

One day while I was sitting in the dayroom watching television, this miserable correctional officer approached me and said, "You need to move that couch back, so the person in the bubble can shoot you in case you do something you have no business doing." (The bubble is like an indoor watch tower with an armed correctional officer inside of it watching the unit.) At the time, I only had three weeks left on my two year sentence. I got up and walked away, but another woman on the couch got up and moved the couch. I said, "I'm not moving anything so I can be shot." The officer overheard me or possibly she read my lips, and she came back yelling and screaming, and I exchanged words with her. One thing led to another and she told me, "I will box that rag off of your head." I told her, "Handle your business," and raised my fists and started dancing around. (The way I danced around in my boxing stance became a major joke in the penitentiary for years to come.)

Another officer on duty on the dayroom floor overheard the officer's threat to beat me up. The miserable correctional officer gave him eye contact I believe to see if he had her back. I'll never forget his response. He backed away from us, put his back on the wall, spread his legs a little while standing, and folded his hands as if he were telling her she was on her own. She then glanced up at the officer in the bubble, who happened to be a really sweet lady that everybody got along with. She could also hear what the miserable officer said; she looked back at her in a sad way. In a flash second, the miserable officer reverted from a street person who could box back to a person of authority and screamed in my ear at about a two-inch range, "Lock it up!" I started to punch her in the face, but it began to hit me exactly where I was and that it was in a no win situation, so I caught myself. Thank God she didn't put her hands on me because I was OH SO READY!

I went to my cell and was later escorted in handcuffs to see the Sergeant in charge at the Watch Office. For some reason, he sent me back to my cell without sending me to the hole. This officer had been causing a lot of problems in our unit, and I guess the Sergeant believed my account of what happened. I went back to my cell and began to pray. During my first prison commitment I became aware of my writing skills, so I did get something out of it. Due to the fact that I only had three weeks left, and I felt that I was not wrong, I searched the rules and regulations manual for the staff and prisoners of the California Department of Corrections, entitled the Title 15.

I wrote a compelling argument on my behalf, citing the fact that no prisoner NOR correctional staff shall provoke a prisoner. I gave the 602, a written, formal complaint against a correctional staff member, to the miserable officer, and she was supposed to respond in five days. I had only three weeks left on my sentence, so I was really afraid that I wasn't going home. Dancing around the officer in a boxing stance could carry anywhere from six months to two more years added on to my sentence, so I decided to avoid her altogether and not leave my cell at all anymore.

The night before it was time for her to respond to my 602, she searched my cell thoroughly and didn't find anything. I didn't give her any eye contact and didn't say a mumbling word while she searched. I knew that she preyed on women who were easy to set off, and I wasn't going to let her trap me twice. The next evening I still didn't come out of my cell on her shift. After the whole unit was locked down for the night, my cell door was popped open and in she came. Oh my God! My stomach did a double flip because I didn't know what this woman was going to pull. She told me, "If you drop that 602 on me, I'll drop that 115 on you." (A 115 is a formal, written complaint against a prisoner.) She went on to smile at me and say, "You are a little person, but you are mighty with the pen." I was relieved and ready to call a truce. I let her know, "I mailed a letter to my grandmother tonight telling her to get in contact with the Watch Commander because I am afraid to leave my cell and in fear for my life, so you probably would want to get it out of the mailbox." She responded, "Is it in the mailbox right now?" I said, "Yeah." She went and got the letter out of the mailbox and tore it in pieces. We were cool from that point on.

Chapter Eleven: It's Time to Get Pretty!

Once I was released, I went back to my old behavior, but I now had a savior that wouldn't allow me to get totally run down. His name was Uncle Parole, and I slowly but surely became dependent upon him to bring me back to my senses. I can remember one time when I was on the bus back to prison from the county jail (I'm not sure if it was my second, third or fourth trip), but I can clearly remember being happy and saying, "It's time to get pretty!"

I knew that although I would be locked up, I would be able to access necessary health procedures such as a pap smear and dental work, while at the same time get sleep, food and peace of mind. People would like to downplay the prison healthcare system, but it was a much better system than what I had on the streets, which was no healthcare system. My overall well-being was much better off in prison than on the streets. In addition to the above-mentioned perks, I was also allowed to look at myself in the mirror and feel pretty, something I didn't feel on the streets.

Besides being healthier and prettier in prison than I was on the streets, I had much more respect. People respected my opinion and took me seriously when I was in prison. Who cares what a crackhead is feeling? In prison I had a higher status, and I am not alone. For example, there was one woman who was so intelligent that rumor has it she was able to write herself off of a life sentence. She had a way with the pen like no other, and she was a penitentiary regular. Many came to her for legal advice. However, on the streets she lived under a bridge. My life in the free world wasn't ideal either. Due to my addiction, I didn't have the capability to think logically, and I had lost connection with my family and children.

There were a few older women who were motherly figures to me throughout the years I spent incarcerated. That was another important missing factor that prison and jail had to offer me that I didn't have access to on the streets, a mom. A couple of my jailhouse moms stand out from the rest. There was a woman I met in the county jail whom I will call Nadine who really took to me for some reason although her biological daughter was incarcerated with us as well. I grew to really care about Nadine because she had a wonderful personality, listened to things I had to say, and kept me laughing. (Laughter and a good sense of humor are key elements to being able to mentally adapt to being locked up.)

One day the food trays arrived, and I asked Nadine what we were having for dinner, and she screamed "Chicken!!!" (Meat is something that was rarely served in the county jail, and chicken was the only form of pure meat that was served.) Nadine started bobbing her head, clucking and walking around in a circle like a chicken. I joined her because I was hungry. When Nadine got closer to the trays, she found out that the chicken trays were for people who had special diets, and the regular trays had what would be considered mush on them. We were embarrassed because some of the other inmates saw how we acted, so we got out of the chow line and walked over to Nadine's bunk doubled over in laughter. Nadine's daughter informed me when I saw her on the streets about six months later that Nadine had died of cancer.

One woman whom I will refer to as Olivia was another one of my jailhouse moms that I got attached to during one of my prison trips for a parole violation. (Out of the five times I went to prison, four of them were for violation of parole.) I knew Olivia from previous county jail trips; she was one of the older women who used to try to calm me down because I was always fighting when I went to the county jail. There was one occasion in the county jail when I was seven months pregnant and almost got into an altercation with another pregnant woman. When I was about to get my treats that I ordered from the commissary cart, the other pregnant woman stepped in front of me and told the commissary cart worker, "This is a stick-up."

I was as irritated by her actions as I was the lack of air and food to support my pregnancy, and we ended up squaring off to fight. When I get ready to fight, I tend to talk to my intended opponent. As we squared off, I started talking. I told her, "I am about to whoop your ass, give you a miscarriage, and then spank your baby." Olivia screamed in a high-pitched voice, "Don't spank the baby!" Everybody started laughing. I swung at the other pregnant woman anyway, and the deputy caught my fist and defused the situation.

A few years later, Olivia, my prison mom, and I lived in Unit 2 together at Northern California Women's Facility, which was a unit that housed parole violators. Parole violators were only allowed to spend two hours per day outside of their cells, so I became really close with Olivia because of all the time we spent together. Neither one of us had any money on our books, nor did we have prison jobs yet because we had just arrived. However, Olivia was quite popular and a lot of the women in the prison liked her, so she was able to collect care packages containing food and hygiene products from different women, and she shared these care packages with me.

When all of the food was gone, we both began to hope and literally pray that someone would answer the letters that we sent to the streets and send some money. I made up a remix to Boyz 2 Men's song "End of the Road." There is a part in that song when one of members of the group starts talking and basically pleading. I changed the words, and every day when the mail was being passed out, I would start pleading for mail to the beat of "End of the Road." Olivia would be cracking up and adding in adlibs to the song. However, every day when the mail was delivered, our cell was passed up. We were starving. When you are coming off of drugs, you're extremely hungry. Those little food trays and small serving sizes just weren't cutting it.

Finally, the correctional officer came to our cell door and delivered a letter to Olivia, and there was a $50 receipt inside. We both got excited, and I asked her where the money came from. She responded while doing a little dance, "The white girl downstairs, bitch!" (The white girl downstairs was an elderly white woman who was attracted to Olivia, so she arranged for the money to be sent. The word "bitch" was referring to me, but it wasn't meant to be offensive.) I started dancing and repeating, "The white girl downstairs, bitch." We both chanted over and over to a beat we created, "The white girl downstairs, bitch," and danced around the cell happy as ever. When Olivia was able to spend the money she got from the white girl downstairs, she made sure I was taken care of. To this very day, whenever I see Olivia I start singing, "The White Girl Downstairs, Bitch." I have seen her in the grocery store and bust out singing that song. That is our permanent, inside joke, and she loves it when I do that. That is my way of showing her that I will always appreciate her feeding me when I was at my worst.

Some of the most sensitive and talented women I know I met in the penitentiary. There were actresses, comedians, singers, dancers, lawyers, etc. Most of them were addicts and therefore were totally different beings in the streets. Despite the rumors, drugs cost a fortune in prison and most addicts do not have the money to buy drugs in prison because their hustling capacities have been cut drastically, so many of the prisoners were at their best physically and mentally.

Recidivism, the cycle of going back and forth to jail, is an easy cycle to fall into. Look at my what jail and prison had to offer me: I was able to get my mind back functioning properly and to regain the ability to THINK FREELY; my sense of humor was restored; my strength, beauty and normal body functions, such as using the bathroom regularly, returned; I received my due respect, and I was able to receive motherly-type attention I never experienced on the streets.

Chapter Twelve: The County

The waiting periods in between the county jail and prison became unbearable once I had been to prison. When I did time in the San Francisco County jail, I was literally behind bars. There was no yard to go to; the only air we received came in through small windows. I was very angry in the county jail, and as a result, I fought ALL of the time. Being respectful and true to your word are of utmost importance in the pen, and therefore, I didn't run into all of the petty situations I encountered while I was in the county jail. Prison was much more spacious in comparison to the county jail, and I would look forward to the bus coming to get me.

After going to prison, the county jail felt like a circus filled with newly detoxing addicts and other weirdos. I was pregnant a few times in the county jail, and I was miserable and evil, so it didn't take much to get under my skin. On one occasion, I got into it with a woman with mental health issues. The county jail was very overcrowded. The cells were supposed to hold eight women. There were eight metal beds in the room, four top bunks and four bottom bunks. However, this particular time there were nine of us in the cell. One mattress was on the floor in between two of the bunks in the rear of the cell. A woman whom we named Ballerina because she walked on her toes all of the time was on the mattress on the floor. We were supposed to be cleaning up because it was time to double-scrub, which means it was time to clean the cell extra good. Therefore, Ballerina's mattress had to be removed from the floor. Ballerina became upset and made the mistake of purposely kicking me in the stomach while she was sitting on the mattress on the floor. I was seven months pregnant at the time.

When she kicked me, everybody in the cell got upset and tried to charge her, but me being the angry fool I was, I wanted to fight her myself. I asked everybody to get back, and "Please let me get her!" I beat her up, picked her up, and literally threw her out of the cell onto the dayroom floor. I shouted to the deputies, "Come get this bitch!" I didn't get put on lockdown because everybody vouched for me and explained that the woman kicked me in the stomach.

I had so many physical altercations in the county jail that the Sergeant housed me in a cell with a convicted arsonist. The Sergeant also pulled me to the side and told me in so many words that she didn't care that I was pregnant and that "...somebody was going to whoop my ass someday." The arsonist was on the top bunk, and I was on the bottom. Every night the arsonist would throw lit matches down to the floor. I have not been able to sleep securely since being housed with this nutcase. To this very day, I wake up about every two hours just to check my surroundings.

Another issue that becomes a factor in the county jail is that people are constantly coming in from the streets with drugs, and for many folks it is hard to resist at such early stages of sobriety. I can remember the one time I used crack while I was in the county jail. A few of us, I believe four, went in together to get the dope. Someone knew how to make a crack pipe out of a tampon, and I took the few little dollars I had in my pocket and bought a microscopic piece of crack. I am still waiting on the smoke because it was so little. To make a long story short, not one of us got high.

There was one woman in the cell who was kicking heroin. It was so funny because the nurse came up to the cell to offer medications to people who had a headache, cold or other ailments. The woman who was kicking heroin must have missed the smoke from her hit too because she didn't stop burning the tampon and holding it up to her mouth even when the jail nurse was present. The nurse just ignored her, but we all laughed. We were all disgusted with ourselves because we were hungry when the commissary cart came around selling goodies, and we had blown our money. That was the first and last time I smoked crack while locked up because I felt too ridiculous when the dope was gone, and I had no resources to get more. I never did that again; the next time I did run across some crack was in prison, and I gave it away. I wasn't about to be sitting up looking stupid.

It is a shame that my life had gone so wrong that prison was something I hoped for. The county jail wasn't the only place where I looked forward to going back to prison. Freedom is a state of being that most animals want to have instinctively, but there were segments of time that I wanted to go back to prison from the free world, and it was not only when I ran out of crack. Sometimes I was just tired of smoking crack, and prison would come to mind as a way out.

One time I left my unit in the Hayes Valley projects and sat on the front stairs of the entire compound by the bus stop. It was a late night (1 or 2 a.m.), but the area was well lit by streetlights. I pulled my crack pipe and dope out of my pockets, set them in a visible area next to me, and shouted, "Here I go!" There was not a soul visible out there, but I was talking to someone, my good 'ole, life-saving Uncle Parole. I knew he wouldn't leave me out there in the wilderness for too long.

Eventually, Hayes Valley North was condemned. The place was filthy, and it was rat infested. The Salvation Army sent staff members around to help the tenants get ready to relocate. I was always getting high and was behind in my rent for a couple of months, so I avoided the Salvation Army people. Whenever they would knock on my door, I looked out the peephole and whispered to my company, "Shhhh...Be quiet, it's the Salvation Army bitches." This went on for a period of time. Finally, I opened the door for them and found out they were trying to help me. I signed some paperwork for relocation services and to get assistance paying my back rent.

That following evening, I had been getting high, and I decided to take a walk up the hill to Page Street projects. There was this Asian man who kept driving around the block. I went to his car to see what he was looking for. He was trying to buy sex. I was trying to get high, so I got in. To be honest, I didn't intend on having sex. I intended on taking his money. However, something felt weird about him, so I spoke with him as if I were being taped. He drove a few blocks and stopped in front of a police car and told me I was under arrest. The case was dropped because we didn't make any type of agreement, but I went back to prison on a parole violation for absconding.

Chapter Thirteen: Becoming Weary

Despite the fact I had grown to NEED prison, a couple of events that happened while I was in prison led me to start thinking about the vicious cycle of smoking crack and getting locked up. I began to feel powerless. One day while I was in my cell in Stockton (I can't remember which prison trip it was, but it wasn't the first one), my cell door was popped open and I was told to report to the Watch Office. When I got there, I saw my attorney for the daughter that was taken away from me at birth, my third child. He gave me some paperwork that said my parental rights were about to be terminated. He also told me that I could look for my daughter when she was 18 years old; she was three years old at the time. Another part of me died that day, the part that believed that one day my life would get better.

There was another significant event that triggered me to question why I was patronizing the criminal justice system. As I mentioned previously, my grandmother was my codependent, but most importantly she was the only person in the world who hadn't given up on me, besides my children. I took her love for granted because it was unearned, and she was able to display it even when I was in my worst condition. On my last prison trip, she became seriously ill. It dawned on me that I needed to make some changes for the better because I could no longer rely on someone to pick me up when I had fallen. I wasn't sure if she was going to live or die, and I was in a horrible mood.

I was in my housing unit and a correctional officer tried to make a wisecrack to me. I told him I wasn't in the mood for that shit. He asked me what was wrong, and I told him my grandmother was in the hospital. He asked me if I wanted to speak to her. I was surprised because this guy was normally an asshole, but he walked me to the Watch Office and helped me to make the call to the hospital. When my grandmother answered the phone, she sounded very feeble. I was used to a strong sounding woman. I felt even feebler than she sounded because there was NOTHING I could do. I couldn't make anything up to her because I was locked up, and I couldn't even so much as see her. I felt really dry and empty on the inside. I began to take a closer look at my prison environment and came to the conclusion that all of the fences and security precautions that were being taken to ensure I remained locked up were in place to protect me from myself.

Whenever someone violates parole, they receive a written report of why they have violated their parole. During my last trip when I got the list of reasons, one stood out from the rest. It said I was "a threat to self and others." To be honest with you, I didn't give a damn about the threat to others part, but the "threat to self" part was felt deep within. I suppose those words were on all of my parole violation reports, but on this occasion I began to dissect what that meant. I can remember going out to the yard after reading the report and looking at the fences in a new way. I told myself, "Those fences are here to protect me from me."

I've always been sort of a clown, meaning I like to make people laugh, and often I make people laugh without trying to. That is why a lot of teachers didn't like me in school. After I received the revelation that I needed the State of California to protect me from myself, I started playing a game at night when we were all locked in our cells. In order to have your cell unlocked by the officer working in the bubble in prison, you had to flag your door. You flagged your door to eat and participate in yard and recreational time. Flagging your door was a term used for taking a nice-sized piece of cardboard from a box, inserting it in an opening from the wall to the door from the inside, and moving it up and down. Note: these pieces of cardboard boxes are not provided by the State; one must look for one on the prison grounds.

Late at night after we were all locked in our cells I began to start clowning. I made a loud announcement as if I were the officer in the bubble that could be heard by anyone who was still awake. I announced loudly, "If you didn't catch a new case, and you are in here for merely being ugly, flag your doors." I was in the parole violator unit. None of us were there for being convicted of new crime in court, which we referred to as "catching a new case"; we were all there because we violated conditions of our parole. To my surprise, a lot of the prisoners began to flag their doors. The officer in the bubble was puzzled and made an announcement over the loud speaker asking why everyone was flagging their doors. We all started cracking up. Mind you, it was about 1 a.m., and we were well outside of the schedule for flagging our doors.

I made a few more announcements such as, "If you are here because you hurt yourself and no one else, flag your door." Again, I got a lot of responses with women flagging their doors. The officer in the bubble then said, "Stop flagging your doors!" We fell out laughing and ceased flagging our doors. Although it was a joke, I was dead serious about what I was saying. I just found a comical way to deal with it.

Chapter Fourteen: The Miracle

When I paroled the last time (which was the 5th time), I went right back to the crack pipe. However, during the last two weeks of my addiction, I began to pray differently. I was truly tired, but I just couldn't seem to do anything right. One day I asked myself, "What do I really want God to do for me?" I then realized that what I wanted was to think differently. I asked God, "Please change the way I think." He heard my cry and opened my eyes. I was able to think clearly about what I was doing to myself from a more rational perspective. For example, one morning during this time period, I went outside. One of my crack cousins was outside, and she gave me some crack and a few dollars. Normally this would make me happy, but this particular time I told myself, "This is going to mess up my whole day."

In addition, I became extremely aware of the dangers I was subjecting myself to and began to rightfully fear for my life during this two-week period. I would have thoughts of myself dying a crackhead. These thoughts really scared me because I believed how I died would be how I would be remembered. I believed my kids would be cursed with that memory. Somehow I was able to feel death; the sky didn't feel that high anymore. It felt as if something deadly was hovering over and around me, slowly but surely invading the space I was allotted on this earth. Death was imminent if I didn't change. There was a series of events that happened that confirmed to me that my life was on borrowed time, but one incident stands out from the rest.

A white guy drove up in the wee hours of the morning looking for drugs. Of course, I didn't have any, but I knew where to get some. I was hoping I could swindle him out of something. Evidently we were both on the same page because after the deal went down I had a piece of newspaper in my hand that he passed as money. I demanded the money, and he proceeded to drive off with me hanging on to the side of his car. He pulled out a huge butcher knife and began to stab at my face. I have never admitted the next part of this story to anyone, but I believe I need to keep it real. While hanging on to his speeding car, I asked the guy if he could please just leave me a piece of the dope for myself if he didn't have any money. He continued to stab at my face, and I finally pleaded with him to stop the car so that I wouldn't hurt myself. He did, and I made it out of that situation with only a small knick on my forehead. I was very upset by the incident (although not upset enough to quit smoking crack that night). My reason for being upset had taken a new twist, though. I wasn't upset because I was unable to get more drugs. I was upset at myself for putting my LIFE on the line for drugs, something I never considered prior to this incident.

This was not the first time I had an encounter with white men coming through the hood being scandalous and attempting to purchase crack. There were a few other times, but there is another incident that comes to mind, and it is pretty humorous, so I feel the need to include the encounter even though it does not fit into the time frame that we are currently in. While reading my accounts of my life, please be advised that my brain has selectively chosen to not remember everything. I believe if I were able to remember everything it would be too painful and overwhelming. However, the death of Whitney Houston in 2012 triggered my memory about something that happened in the 1990's, and I feel this story needs to be included.

About a year prior to having my life damn near taken by a desperate white man who was addicted to crack, I had another encounter with a white man, also a crackhead, who was unable to accept that fact that all of his money was spent. Again, it was in the wee hours of the morning (2 a.m. – 4 a.m.). I was broke, but I was not sleepy. I was in the company of a woman that was known by the name of Butt Naked. Despite the fact that most sane people were asleep, I was wide awake, and I constantly made a loud spoken announcement during this time period that I wasn't sleepy and was going to "check the perimeter" to see if I could get some more dope.

Butt Naked agreed she was not sleepy either, so we decided to make one last attempt to check the perimeter. When I said I wanted to check the perimeter, that meant I was going to walk all over the projects I lived in to see if there were any prospects to get some more crack. When Butt Naked and I got to the middle of the perimeter, a vehicle pulled up, and we approached it to see what the person wanted. It was a white man in a truck, and he said that he was trying to find some crack. We told him we didn't have any.

About 15 minutes later, he came through again. Again, we told him we didn't have any crack and didn't know where to get any. After the second time, being the crackhead I was, I said, "If he comes back, I am going to get him." I started looking on the ground to see what I could make look like crack in order to get his money. I was able to find pieces of eggshells and also was able to find clear plastic. I broke the eggshells down and wrapped it inside clear plastic and burned the tips of the plastic to make it look the way crack looked when it was sold.

I told Butt Naked, "If he comes back, I am going to sell him this. I told him twice I didn't have anything." Lo and behold, about two minutes later the same white truck came through. I lied and said I found somebody with some dope, and I instructed him to hurry up and give me the money. I handed him the fake package I had prepared and collected what I thought was money, and we both, Butt Naked and myself, ran back to my apartment/project afterwards.

When we got in the unit, we were laughing, and I felt relaxed and relieved that I had some dope money, so I turned on my radio in order to unwind. I reached in my pocket to retrieve the money and found out that the white man gave me pieces of newspaper strippings instead of money. While all of this was going on, Whitney Houston's record "Shoop" from the *Waiting to Exhale* soundtrack came on, and she was singing like an angel without a worry in the world. I began to talk to the radio and Whitney, saying things like, "Shoop, my ass," "Do you have some crack?" and "This bitch is shooping, and I just sold eggshells for newspaper." We laughed so hard we cried. Humor is one of the reasons I am still alive. Although I was able to laugh, I wonder what the white man who risked his life coming through the hood felt like when he figured out he traded newspaper for eggshells. I'm sure he didn't have Whitney to comfort him. RIP, WHITNEY HOUSTON; THANK YOU FOR YOUR VOICE AND COMFORT!!

Getting back to the last two weeks of my crack tribulations, an Asian guy claimed he wanted to turn a date, in other words, trade sex for money. I didn't have any resources at the time, so I followed him to an empty construction site that is now a convalescent home. When we got there, he wrapped his hands around my neck and proceeded to choke me. I screamed, "Jesus," and the guy loosened up and let me go. I guess he had some type of connection to Jesus, thank God! I truly believed my days on this earth were numbered. It felt like something really dark and dreary was traveling near me. I couldn't see it, but I know it was death. I could feel it and half way think my way through what it would mean. I credit my ability to acknowledge my own death was soon to come to the prayer I mentioned previously.

On January 7, 1997, at approximately 3 a.m., I smashed my crack pipe (for the millionth time) and went to sleep. When I woke up that morning, I was crying and thanking God at the top of my voice. I didn't know what I was thanking God for at that time, but I am well aware today. I didn't touch a crack pipe for the next nine and a half years from that day. I don't know exactly what happened, but I do believe God was responsible and the transformation took place in my sleep.

Up until this point, I had not been to see my parole officer. I walked away from the house I had been getting high in and contacted him. I told him I needed help. He told me to come see him, and I went, which was way out of my character. (I had not reported to my parole officer in months, so there must have been some type of divine intervention.) There was a program for parolees, and the woman I had been getting high with had a bed waiting for her, but she kept setting back the date. I remember halfheartedly telling her, "I am going to take your bed if you don't get out of here." When I got to the parole office, my parole agent explained to me that there was one bed at this program, but someone was supposed to come get it at 1 p.m. He told me this was her last chance and to come back at 1 p.m. I knew who she was, and I also knew she wasn't coming.

I didn't have any money or many options, so I walked back to the community I was most comfortable in. It was about 9 a.m. when I left the parole office, and 1 p.m. was a long time from then, but somehow all of the circumstances of that day fell perfectly into place. On my way back I saw this sweet, wholesome looking, elderly white woman. I had never seen her before in my life. I screamed to her, "I am getting ready to go to a program and change my life!" She replied, "Here, you're going to need this." She gave me a cold cheeseburger on a French roll. With every bite I took of that burger I began to think clearer. I thought to myself, "She was right." I later came to believe that woman was an angel.

When I got back to one of the crack spots I used to visit, everybody was asleep, so I left. It was a rare occasion to find everyone sleeping in a crack house. I went outside in front of the crack spot and began watching the cars that passed by. I saw a green and gold Jeep Cherokee, and I told the person who was standing next to me, "I like that car." I realized I hadn't liked anything but crack cocaine for quite a long time, and I felt empowered. I gained the strength to walk away. I got on the bus, and went home to get some clothes. I told the bus driver that I was going to a program, and she let me on the bus for free, gave me a transfer, and wished me good luck. I made it back to the program at 1 p.m., and of course, the woman who the bed was reserved for didn't show up.

Chapter Fifteen: Maintaining

I stayed at the program for parolees for a couple of months, but I didn't make any preparations for the care of my housing unit. When I was released from prison for the last time, I received a one bedroom unit in the Sunnydale Housing Project. I was in a one bedroom in Sunnydale because I no longer had my children, and the public housing site I was living in prior to my last prison trip, Hayes Valley, was in the process of being torn down and rebuilt. Fortunately, I signed the paperwork with the Salvation Army for relocation services the before I was arrested, and that sealed the deal for me to be able to have another public housing unit upon my release.

I left a drug dealer in my unit in Sunnydale without telling him I was leaving because I didn't know I was leaving; it was a spur of the moment thing. He left a pitbull in the apartment, and dogs were not allowed in the public housing site I lived in. I was told by one of the neighbors I had keeping an eye on my unit that the windows had been boarded up, and the SPCA took a dog away. When I called the public housing office from the drug program, I was told if I didn't come home, the unit would be reported as abandoned. I told my counselor at the program the circumstances, and he wasn't very understanding. He told me I needed to choose between my recovery and my housing unit. I told him my housing unit was my recovery. I couldn't afford to live anywhere else in San Francisco but the projects. And due to my immature behavior that I often displayed while in the program, I didn't feel comfortable relying solely upon them for refuge; I could have been put out at any given moment.

When I discussed my choices with grandmother, she replied, "If you give up your housing, you will be hooome LESS, and you don't want to be LESS anything." She made a point of stretching the word homeless into two words by pausing in between, so I would understand her point. My grandmother was the wisest person I knew, so I left the program the next morning.

While I was in the program, I met the man I later married, had my 5th child by, and eventually separated from. He was in trouble because of his temper while at the program, and coincidentally the staff voted to throw him out the very same afternoon that I left the program, so he ended up living with me. With my future husband, I returned to a one-bedroom public housing unit located right next door to the crack house in the Sunnydale housing projects. Somehow very early in our recovery we were able to cope with going right back to the same unit I used dope in. Even though we could hear the gate that was attached to the front door of the crack house next door to us swinging back and forth all hours of the day and night, we somehow remained crack-free. This relationship lasted for about five years. I wish I was open to discussing my ex-husband and the years we spent together because he was very supportive in my growth to some degree. However, to date, I can't stand the guy.

Not only did we live next door to a crack house, there were several others in the immediate area, not to mention a parking lot right up the hill where crack could easily be purchased all hours of the day and night. Living in public housing in Sunnydale was quite a different experience than living in Hayes Valley. Sunnydale had blocks and blocks of public housing units. The only stores that were in the immediate vicinity were liquor stores. Groceries stores were very far away; crack was more accessible than groceries. The bus didn't run as often in Sunnydale as it did in Hayes Valley, and many of the bus drivers ended their routes prematurely before reaching the projects. Trying to remain clean and sober while being literally stranded in a drug and alcohol infested, vitamin and mineral absent, violent environment required a lot of determination, overlooking, and downright luck.

When I first came home from the program for parolees, I was assigned to a new parole officer from the high-risk unit; I was considered high-risk because I rarely reported to the parole department in the past. My new parole agent was on my every move and would sometimes show up at my house at 6 a.m. to drug test me. One good thing he did was give me a referral for a job that was supposed to last for a couple of days but ended up lasting two months. I worked for a Jewish deli as a dishwasher and was paid $5 per hour in cash. My boss was a very sweet woman. I worked closely with an Asian man who would frequently get mad at me because I had no dishwasher experience, and he thought I was unqualified for the job. This job lasted until a woman who had been injured on the job returned to work.

Two of my children, my 8-year-old son and my 12-year-old daughter were returned to me for the umpteenth time. This time was easier to get them back because CPS wasn't involved. The last time they were removed from me, I requested their family members to come get them. When their family members attempted to call CPS on me, the CPS worker who was contacted told the family that I had a right to have my children cared for by somebody else if I was unable. They were advised to call CPS back if I returned and was still unfit. We were all (my future husband, my two children and myself) living in a one bedroom project in Sunnydale.

I then found a job working as an interviewer who conducted phone surveys on health issues for a market research group at a pay rate of $7 per hour with no benefits. Although I was often criticized for my aggressive demeanor when my phone calls were monitored, I was one of the top interviewers in the company in regards to the number of people I was able to convince to participate, so eventually the criticism stopped. While I worked on this job, I became pregnant with and gave birth to my fifth child, Andre; he was born nine years and one day later than my last child. This would be the first child that I kept custody of from the beginning to date. I was thrown a very nice surprise baby shower by my job for Andre, and I returned back to work as a market research interviewer after he was born.

Although my job as an interviewer wasn't a very good job and didn't have any benefits, I learned valuable skills such as the ability to talk to people from all walks of life. I also taught myself how to use the 10-key pad by sight, a skill that led into another temporary job at the Pacific Stock Exchange for $10 an hour and still no benefits. I later participated in a job fair for convicted felons. A certain hotel chain was there. I applied and was hired for the position of reservationist at $9 an hour with health benefits. I didn't like working as a reservationist; it was really shady, and I felt I had to use some of the skills that I used to get drugs, which involved trickery. For example, if a senior citizen called in and asked for the senior's rate, we were instructed to give it to them even though there may have been a better rate available that day. In addition, the manager had a habit of treating me like a little girl and would often openly scold me in front of others even though I was the oldest on the job site.

Living in Sunnydale was getting to be very hard. The unit was very crowded, and I was expecting a new baby. And to top it off, there was a war going on between up the hill and down the hill. We lived in between, so it was constant gunfire. I had been receiving mail from the new Hayes Valley North projects because they were almost completely redeveloped. I applied to return, and we received a three bedroom public housing unit. Although it was public housing, we had three stories, a one-car garage, wall to wall carpeting, etc. And I was returning to Fillmoe where I was born and raised, could move around much better, and felt more comfortable. Plus, my grandmother lived around the corner from where I was moving back to.

After we moved back to The Valley, I received a flyer in my mailbox from Jewish Vocational Services, a non-profit agency that helped people become self-sufficient. I cannot remember what the flyer said, but I do remember the word "career" was used within the text. That word caught my eye. Up until this point, I just wanted a job and to be able to feed my kids. I'd never thought of myself as having a career. I was fascinated by the thought, so I followed up and began working with the agency that sent me the flyer.

This agency treated me with the utmost respect, and this includes all staff ranging from the receptionist, counselors, and directors. This was something I was unaccustomed to, especially when dealing with an agency that dealt with the so-called underprivileged. (I hate the word "underprivileged" because it is a white defined word. I believe it is a privilege to have melanin in my skin that prevents me from wrinkling, and thus keeps me young looking. In addition, the prefix of the word insinuates I am beneath something or somebody. If I am under, there must be something over.)

I became really close with my caseworkers at this new program. I went to the program daily after work at the Stock Exchange, worked on my computer skills, and applied for positions while I was prepped for interviews and encouraged by a group of amazingly sincere women. I explained to them that I wanted to seek out meaningful employment because I was turned off by the reservationist work. I began to look for jobs in the non-profit/health sector. Finally, after two years of struggling due to my record and sporadic employment history, I landed a decent job as a data entry operator for a well-known teaching hospital; I started at $14.83 an hour and had excellent benefits for me and all of my children. Before I got this job, I was just about ready to give up. Prior to my interactions with the group of women at Jewish Vocational Services who seemed to recognize and respect my intelligence, I was satisfied with the basics in life and did not recognize my own abilities. I feel really grateful to have had that good experience with them. They helped me lift the bar.

Chapter Sixteen: College?

For my new position, I worked as a data entry operator for a phone line that was used by health care providers when they had questions about their HIV positive patients. I was responsible for typing in the questions and answers for the nation's most complex HIV medical issues, and I learned a great deal of information. I became close with some of the physicians and pharmacists that worked on the phone line. During my first few months, I asked several questions, and a couple of the physicians began to teach me about HIV as if I were a medical student. I was taught how the virus attacked, the likelihood of transmission, the effects of HIV antiretroviral medications and many other things. I became a semi-expert. One doctor went as far to say that I knew more about HIV than medical students did after their first year of medical school.

Although I was the only Black person on the job and I didn't have a higher education, my opinion was valued. My opinion was valued to the point to where I had to start reevaluating what I believed I was capable of because I was successfully interacting with people that I considered to be on another level than I was. Before I had the personal experience of knowing and holding conversations with people who had advanced degrees, I thought they were a special type of people.

Every now and then someone on the job, particularly my manager and a pharmacist who worked on the phone line, would suggest that I go to college. I said I would go, but I wasn't really sure. However, one day the manager said something that made a lot of sense to me. My excuse for not going to college was that it was going to take too long because of my parental and work commitments, and I said, "I'll be 50 before I graduate." My manager responded, "Then if you make it to 50 you will have a degree, or you can make it to 50 and still not have one. Time is going to pass regardless, so you might as well make the best of it." That sales pitch worked. I signed up to take the placement tests at the local community college.

I placed high in English and lower than I thought I would in Math. (I didn't know Geometry or Algebra at all; they weren't required for the GED.) I was advised by a counselor to take English or Math first to get it out of the way. I signed up for one class, English 96, as an experiment to see if I would fit in. I was blessed to get a really good instructor who allowed me to be myself on paper. I had been living in public housing for quite a long time, and I wasn't sure if some terms I used were slang or formal English. In addition, I didn't know of anything to write about but ghetto life.

I used to get mixed responses from people outside of school that I would share my essays with. My grandmother used to ask me if I knew of anything else to write about except Black people and Black issues. My first two kids' father, Kookie, who has since died in a car accident, used to get excited when I read him the essays and used to shout, "Keep it Black!" I can still hear his voice whenever I want to water something down that I am writing about my people, which helps me to not sugarcoat our issues. Luckily, the instructor for English 96 appreciated reading about the Black experience and found my papers to be very interesting. He warned me that everyone would not appreciate this type of writing and that I would have to be careful as I moved along my college path.

One day while we were on break the instructor stopped me outside and said, "You are a very gifted writer. You can be whatever you want to be, possibly a lawyer." I thought to myself, "If only he knew who I am," but I could tell by the look in his eyes that he was sincere and tears welled up in my eyes. I thanked him and walked away. These words may not sound like much, but that was just what I needed to hear to determine I was worthy of being in college despite my past. I still to this day have much love for this instructor. I believe had it not been for him, I wouldn't have gone as far as I did with my education. It's not that I couldn't have succeeded without him, but to be honest, there were many teachers that followed him that really irritated me. If they had been involved in my first experience as a college student, I'm not sure I would have gone any further. Therefore, thank you, Mr. Langdon!

Chapter Seventeen: Butterteeth

Another significant event that led me to see that I was holding myself back based upon my own perception of who was supposed to be smart was the fact that I allowed myself to receive training and coaching from a white man who was also in my first college class. Although I never asked him for any help, this man would volunteer to come over to my desk and help me. He was a middle-aged, heavy set, greasy-haired white man who had a terrible odor and a buttery film all over his teeth. Despite all of his negative traits, he had the ability to speak as if he were very intelligent, so I stomached the tutoring and advice because I assumed he was smarter than I was.

One day we were asked to switch papers and evaluate each other's writings. Of course, Butterteeth came over to my desk so that he could help me out, and I was willing. When we switched papers, I couldn't make hide nor hair out of what his paper was about; he had horrible writing skills! I was ashamed of myself and made a pact to examine why I assumed that Butterteeth was smarter than I was, which I know now to be internalized racism imposed by society's definition of who is supposed to be smart and who isn't.

Little by little I began to recognize how gifted I was scholastically. I was receiving straight A's on all of my papers, and those A's felt better than a crack high, so I pushed myself to get more. I finished my first class with an A grade. Amazingly, the instructor that I was taking was moving on to teach the next level of English,

English 1A, the following semester, and I signed up for his class again, but this time I took a couple of other classes with it. My new English class focused on persuasive writing, and we analyzed very controversial issues such as the death penalty and legalization of drugs. Early on in the class, I had the same experience of people assuming I was dumb, but I had gained confidence in myself and didn't waiver much.

We were assigned to work in groups, and there was this elderly white woman who wanted to take the lead all of the time. She was a self-proclaimed professional children's book writer. While we were in the group, the professional writer and I would disagree on certain English concepts, and the group would choose to follow her lead; however, I would do things on my paper as I knew them to be right and just kept my mouth closed as if I were doing what she said. I was not going to make the same assumption with her as I did with Butterteeth. This woman constantly challenged me, and it became very hard to deal with her, but I held my composure. I studied too hard to worry about what she was talking about. I learned to trust my mind.

After time went by, the self-proclaimed professional writer approached me and asked me, "What grade did you get on that last paper?" I responded, "An A." She went on to say, "What about the paper before that?" I responded, "An A." She asked, "Do you get all A's?" I said, "Yes." She admitted to me that she was having trouble in the class and asked if I would proofread her papers before she turned them in. I agreed to help her and gave her some tips.

Another uncomfortable part of the class was the debates we had about the issues we were analyzing. People tended to challenge my opinion very often. It was weird because all of the students voiced their opinions, but my opinion had to be challenged for some reason. I found out that I thought very differently on controversial topics than a lot of the other students did. It was hard to hear their opinions on certain topics, so I spoke up, and then I felt attacked because it wasn't just one student going against me; it was several students debating with me at one time. Learning how to debate on this level was extremely challenging. Where I lived, the argument wouldn't go on for that long without someone getting slapped. Despite this fact, I couldn't hold my tongue; however, I managed to make it through and receive an A.

Chapter Eighteen: Looking for My Purpose

While going to school, I still had the job at the research hospital, and I noticed that a vast number of the calls that were placed at the phone line were in regards to Black patients. I was unaware of the disproportionate level of HIV among Black people at the time. Due to the high number of Black people affected, I decided to take some HIV/AIDS Prevention Education courses because they were also transferable if I decided to go on and pursue a Bachelors Degree. In addition to my general education courses, I began taking courses in the HIV Prevention Certificate Program.

As I mentioned previously, it was the number of Black patients who were inquired about that made me seek out the HIV field, but I was in no way prepared for the statistics and hopeless teaching strategies that were to take place. The instructors introduced one Black statistic after another. For example, we were introduced to data that found that Black youth were more promiscuous than white youth; we were told that Black women represented the fastest growing group for HIV infection in the country, and Black people represented ½ of the newly diagnosed HIV cases in the country. We also were introduced to the theory that HIV came from African monkeys, the Africans were eating the monkeys and this is how they became infected. The down low concept was also emphasized as a way the virus is passed in the Black community; there was no name for the white men who may happen to hide their sexuality from their partners, and I knew they had to exist.

I was extremely disgusted with the information. The Jewish female instructor delivered these statistics in a matter-of-fact, that's the way it is type manner. There was not a hint of sadness relayed in her voice or in her facial expressions when she delivered these messages, and there was no mention of what could be done about it. I wondered if she would have been talking about Jewish people if she would have discussed these issues in such a nonchalant manner. These statistics were overwhelming. I guess I was supposed to be used to hearing this type of information, but I wasn't. I was taught as a young child that being Black was a special, powerful experience and that I should be proud to be Black. What I was hearing and feeling in the classroom was just the opposite. I was very disturbed and distraught. I began to feel as if I was fighting a losing battle, and I expressed this to a couple of the instructors in the program.

My reactions to their teaching strategies were met different ways. One teacher, the Jewish woman, told me maybe I had chosen the wrong field because that's the way things are. If I was willing to accept the way things were, I wouldn't have chosen to take HIV prevention courses. I was there to learn how to make change not accept things the way they were. I was somehow expected to remain in this field and be content with what I was hearing. I began to reject all of the concepts I learned, especially the concept of a theory. I figured if their theories were so valid, why are we so sick? I couldn't understand why a Black woman who lived in a primarily Black setting in San Francisco, public housing, had to come all the way to college to hear the news about her own community from white people.

I found that I was not able to sit in class and listen to these hopeless statistics and not do anything. I began to take action. I worked on the Speakers' Bureau, giving speeches to other classes about HIV; I created a free condom distribution network with businesses that catered to a primarily Black clientele in the Western Addition of San Francisco (Fillmoe), and I developed HIV informational meetings in public housing sites in San Francisco, targeting Black women who lived there. In addition, I made a very important decision to pursue a Bachelors of Science in Health Education with an emphasis in Community Based Public Health.

Chapter Nineteen: Graduation

I continued to do well in all of my studies, and earned straight A's in the classes I took at the community college level, except for two B's. In one class, I got a B because I just didn't put my all in the class. The teacher was boring and read everything he talked about from a book. I hated the class, and it was a basic health prevention class. I knew the information from the class like the back of my hand, but I just couldn't get into it.

The other class I received a B in was a Speech class. It didn't matter how hard I tried, I still couldn't get an A in that class. I think it was because I refused to talk like a white person. Don't get me wrong, I didn't use slang in my speeches, but I kept the me in my voice; otherwise I would have been stuttering. I don't do well with disguising the Blackness in my voice; I get lost for words during the performance. I gave a speech on affirmative action that drew tears from some of the students in the class, and I was followed all the way from the classroom to my car by white male students still discussing the topic. As a matter of fact, I called home to let everybody know I was being followed to my car by white men in case I didn't make it home. Regardless of the audience reaction, I still got a B.

Despite those two Bs, I received a letter from the Graduation Department saying that my grades made me eligible to give the commencement speech at the graduation. At 39 years old, I was to receive an Associate Degree in Liberal Studies, and I was graduating with a 3.87 GPA. I was asked to prepare a speech and deliver it in front of a committee. Another woman and I tied for first place, and we were both chosen to deliver speeches at the ceremony. It was a big responsibility, and I had to practice with a speech coach.

The day before the gradation, I was called in to speak with the deans. I was scolded about a "threatening email" I wrote to one of the faculty that worked on campus. I had emailed the Speech teacher about how I felt that she discriminated against me. I told the deans I didn't know the content of that email was threatening, and one of them responded, "It is white folks' type of threatening!" That made me think; I didn't know what white folks' type of threatening was. There was one Hispanic dean and one Black dean. All of a sudden, the Hispanic dean said, "How dare you try to screw up this opportunity? No one has ever come from where you come from and delivered this speech! You are breaking the mold!" The Black dean then said, "We are going to give you the opportunity to speak, and you better represent!!! You are going to go on after the other woman; we have changed your slot."

When I left the room, I immediately went home and altered my speech that was to be given in front of 2,000 some odd people at the Masonic Auditorium in San Francisco. Prior to my changing the speech, it was a politically correct, non-heartfelt speech that had become such due to the coaching I was receiving. Here is an excerpt of the actual speech I delivered to the Class of 2004:

I searched my heart to find the message I would like to leave you with today. Who knows the next time I will be able to speak to such a large crowd? Some of us have a rougher time attending college than others. For some, the road to college is a wide road; for others, it is like walking on a tightrope. For some the war in Iraq is the issue of top priority, but for some of us it is the war right outside our doors.

Just the other day my community buried a 17-year-old Black boy who was killed in the streets of San Francisco. Ironically, while we were attending the funeral, another young Black man was killed a few blocks away. I had a final that night, and I couldn't bring myself to concentrate, so I left early. This scenario is just a glimpse of what people living in the ghetto have to endure while pursuing an education. This has been a rough battle, but I had something to prove to society and myself, so I kept climbing. I had to set an example.

Media, where are you? I know you are up in here because the mayor is up in here. I need you to do me a favor because my community is experiencing a lot of disappointments, and we need some good news, so I was sent here to represent. I need you to tell the people that a Black woman, an ex-convict, an ex-addict, living in the projects, graduated with the highest honors this morning...

Throughout my speech I received standing ovations, and it took a lot longer than I had expected. However, the last paragraph that I quoted had the largest reaction. After I said those words, it seemed as if the Holy Ghost took over the place. People started screaming and hollering. The graduates from the Black Student Union were sitting near the stage, and I could hear the young Black men barking, and it seemed as if the stadium was turned upside down with joy for a period of time.

My entire family was there: my grandmother, my husband, my aunt, my cousins, my children, my mom and my sister on my mom's side. It was funny because I have the official video tape of the graduation, but the video that my little cousin taped is dramatic. It has the crowd reaction in the tape. As soon as I said the last quoted paragraph, the camera turned in a full circle and I could see people jumping out of their seats. I asked one of the instructors that I invited to come to my graduation why she thought the crowd reacted like that. She responded, "Because they have never heard anything like that before."

This was the first time in my life that I was able to make so many members of my family proud of me at the same time, and the day that I graduated with an Associate degree was by far the best day of my life! My youngest son Andre, who happened to be five years old at the time, clapped for me and shouted "Mommy!" the entire speech. That night we (my family, friends and neighbors) partied until 4 a.m. Every few hours, I would raise my hands in the air and everyone would cheer, "Yay, Marilyn!" I took full advantage of that, and I had them to do that one final time before I announced I was going to sleep and the party was over around 4 a.m. the morning following the graduation. To this day, people from this community remind me that I am educated and praise me for it.

Chapter Twenty: An Honorable
Mention to the Projects

I have lived in a total of five public housing sites in San Francisco located in Fillmoe and Sunnydale: I lived in Page Street once, Sunnydale twice, and The Valley twice. My stints living in Sunnydale were short lived due to being robbed the first time and being relocated the second time. Page Street is right up the hill from the The Valley, which is located in Fillmoe where I was born and raised. Thus, I spent a great deal of my adult life living within a four block radius. Even though the public housing developments that I have lived in have been drug-infested death traps, I grew to love some of my neighbors. We played together, fought together, fed each other, watched each other's kids, and helped each other out in ways that I would probably not have experienced in a well-off community. Everybody knew everybody. That is one part of living in the projects that I will always miss. My neighbors and I were like family, especially when I moved back to The Valley. All of our kids played together, and I felt well-connected.

I always had someone to talk to, and the humor was ongoing. I can remember one day I was taking a nap about six months after I moved back to The Valley, and my doorbell was ringing non-stop. When I got up and looked out of my window, I looked down into my driveway, and there was a card table with four of my female neighbors playing cards in my driveway. It was a warm day. All of them looked up smiling, and one of them shouted, "Turn on the music!!!" I used to blast my music sometimes, so it could be heard on the block. I could have been mad because they woke me up and had decided to put a card table in my driveway without even asking, but all I could do was laugh and turn the music on.

Hot days were the days we spent the most time together. We would have water fights that lasted until the wee hours of the morning. One time, about forty to fifty of us were outside listening to music and socializing at about 1 o'clock in the morning. There were about five main households who were close, and there were probably 20 kids altogether, plus the kids' friends were also there. The ages in the crowd ranged from 2 – 40 years old; I was the oldest. It was the hottest night of that particular year, and we were having a ball!

The police and housing security guards came and told us we were unfit parents and started to videotape our children and our interactions with them. One of my neighbors told the police, "I am out here with my kids. Do you know what your kids are doing?" The police left, but the security guards kept asking us to go into the house even though there was no violence being committed, and San Francisco didn't and still doesn't have a curfew. We ignored them and continued having fun.

There is another incident that I have to give an honorary mention to. While living in the Valley, I fixed my place up pretty nice, and I got a 50 gallon fish tank that was decorated nicely. However, I had one fish, a Red Devil, which wound up killing all of the other fish, including the algae eaters. One of my neighbors who had moved from The Valley to Page Street was always bragging about how vicious his fish was. I told him, "Don't have me go get my fish!" He replied, "Go get him!"

I drove down the hill and told my kids what he said. One of my sons got a bucket of water, scooped our fish out of the tank with a net, and began walking up the hill to Page Street with the fish in the bucket. My daughter walked up the hill with him; they were teenagers at the time. I drove my car up the hill to meet them. When we got to Page Street, we asked the neighbor's wife where he was, and she asked, "What's goin' on?" We told her why we were there. She said, "Oh, no, y'all didn't come up her like that! Come on!" We followed her to her house, and a few other people also followed. When we all got upstairs, my son poured our fish along with the water from the bucket into the tank with their fish. All of a sudden, their fish started beating the shit out of our fish. I let it go on for about 45 seconds, and then I told my son, "Get my pet out of there!" My son got our fish out of the tank. We laughed, and the husband said, "I told you." We humbly left their house with our fish. I don't think I will ever be able to replace the close-knit bonds I had with my neighbors in The Valley.

Chapter Twenty-one: I am Not
Supposed to Be Here

Although I played around a lot with my neighbors in The Valley and I had a lot of other responsibilities such as work and family, I was somehow able to remain focused and extremely serious about getting a higher education. Due to the fact that I did so well at the community college level, I chose to pursue a Bachelors degree. One of the teachers I had grown very close to suggested I choose Health Education as my major for undergraduate studies. I valued his opinion, so I applied and was accepted. When I got to the university, I couldn't help but notice the diversity at the campus. Among my cohort, there were about five Black women. Two of us were from what would be referred to as the hood, and the other three were middle-class.

Five of us hung out together: a really sweet Eritrean girl who lived around the corner from me; another Eritrean who lived with her parents, who happened to be homeowners in a decent neighborhood of San Francisco; a woman who was raised in the hood but had a long military career and managed to make her way out; and myself, a 40-year-old mother of five, ex-addict, ex-convict, who had lived all of her adult life in public housing.

After class one day, we were all talking, and they were speaking on how they work hard to not be labeled as "ghetto." It was a matter-of-fact conversation, and it wasn't directed towards anyone. Up until that point, I was holding back my "ghettoness" a bit myself, but something clicked inside of me and I responded, "Well, I'm going to tell y'all right now. I'm ghetto as hell. I've been living in the projects for the past 20 years, and I would have to work too hard to not be ghetto, and since I'm not being paid to be here, I'd rather just be myself." I also noted, "But for the records, I am a straight A student."

I was the oldest in the crew. All of the other young women were in their early twenties. One young woman was in her early thirties. I can't describe the look that was on all of their faces. It seemed as if that type of response was not expected at all. We all felt a little uncomfortable for a moment, but they all came to respect me. As it turned out, I was the best writer among my group and got the best grades. By the end of the school year, the crew was all slapping five, laughing loud and acting "ghetto." I guess my statement and unwillingness to change enabled them to loosen up.

The education that I received during this time period sort of took the fire out of my desire to make change. During my first semester, I was a part of a class that studied a research paper entitled "All Our Kin." This research paper was written about the network systems that were used by Black people in the projects. I was offended by the way we (I say we because I was a Black woman living in the projects) were being studied as if we were odd. A couple of students, particularly a young white woman in her early 20's, were simply amazed at how people in the projects hustle beyond their welfare check. To me that was common knowledge. I asked the young lady, "Could you live off of $341 per month?" She replied, "No." I then asked her, "Well, why do you think someone else can?"

The conversation continued, and the students continued commenting on what I considered to be basic information as if they were reading a National Geographic article about an uncivilized tribe. I raised my hand and asked, "Just like you guys find what we do as strange, I've always wondered why the streets are empty in white communities on hot days? We have water fights on hot days. Everyone is out having a ball in my community and your streets our empty. What do y'all do on hot days? That seems strange to me."

At that moment, the air thickened and some white folks became red in the face. I did the unheard of, which was to speak on white folks' personal behaviors as if their behaviors were not the norm. They were being taught that they were overprivileged, and if that was so then their way must be the right way, right? Their way of behaving is not open for discussion. I later found out that Ethnic Studies excludes white folks altogether. The words racism and social justice were commonly used when discussing people of color during my studies, but the role that white folks play in it was not discussed. I felt like the white students got the benefit of talking about and examining Black people as if they were the perfect human beings without having to examine themselves and their actions.

The young white woman who became beet red and very angry said I was stereotyping white people when I questioned their whereabouts on hot days, but it was okay for Black folks to be examined and scrutinized over and over again. Other Black students in the class became a little agitated. One young Black man who was about 19 years old asked the question, "I don't understand why you guys are so intrigued with Black life?"

The teacher, a Hispanic woman, took sides with the white folks unknowingly. She later called me in her office and said she thought I was going to hit someone in that class. She must have not been paying attention to the look on the young white woman's face who was angered to the point her face was beet red, nor must she have paid attention to the malice in the white woman's eyes as she spoke. Somehow, only my words were taken as threatening even though I didn't curse or say I was going to do harm to anyone. The instructor also took the liberty to explain that there was a certain way to conduct ourselves in an academic setting. All I did was challenge the self-proclaimed dominant culture's way of life as a strange one. Instead, they would rather have me to believe I am strange.

I was so frustrated with the concept of research and analyzing findings when it comes to Black folks that I wrote this parable:

A father left two of his sons a home. One of the sons was much more powerful than his brother, so he got greedy and kicked him out of the house and spread lies about him. The other brother went on and made a way for himself despite being cheated out of what was rightfully his. The powerful brother noticed that his brother was still alive, and he asked himself, "I wonder

how he is still making it despite all I have done to him?"
Thus, he decided to STUDY him.

I noticed that much of the curricula in my educational program emphasized people with my characteristics: addicts, dark skinned people, incarcerated people, and overall "ghetto people." I constantly found myself becoming offended and depressed. I asked myself, "Why are you so upset?" Due to the fact that most of what I learned was about my daily struggle, I didn't learn much, and I learned it in a manner that gave me no sense of hope. Equitable solutions were not a common theme to fight the health disparities that exist among people of color. Despite the fact that the data suggests that racism, poverty and lack of education are major root causes for health disparities, none of the strategies suggested to fight these disparities addressed the above-mentioned root causes. Instead, basic, predictable solutions such as Section 8, food stamps, condoms, and clean air were suggested as answers to these issues.

During one of my classes (I believe it was another Ethnic Studies class), I learned that Black people didn't assimilate as well as everyone else in America because we were non-voluntary immigrants. I learned a fact that I already knew, which was all of the other ethnicities came to America by choice for a better life, but Black folks were basically kidnapped. Hearing this out loud in an educational setting didn't make it easier for me to assimilate and talk like the average student of color, whom I perceived to be trying too hard to sound like everyone else. As a matter of fact, hearing this was like watching the segment of the mini-series *Roots* in which massa whopped Kunta Kinte until he said his name was Toby. Although I knew the history, what I learned just didn't sit right. Assimilation didn't make sense to me. If people with my qualities were the ones who were suffering the most, why should I alter myself to the point that they cannot relate to me or I to them after I received the education that I wanted to dedicate to help create change in my own community?

It was then revealed to me what was wrong with the messages that were sent to me through the curricula. It, meaning the curricula, was designed to talk about me, not with me. I WAS NOT SUPPOSED TO BE THERE. All of the talk about "meeting people where they are," a phrase that is frequently used in the public health setting, doesn't apply in areas that would bring about true equality, such as academia. In academia, the instructors too often meet people where they think they are supposed to be.

"Equality" is mentioned and supposedly is the theme of public health, but in my opinion, it is not pursued. "Social justice" is another term that is often thrown around in public health terminology. I believe many people have preconceived notions about what justice is when it concerns certain people. Social justice is not you making sure that people have their basic and minimal needs met; to my understanding, social justice is a call for those that have been excluded to be provided with equal chances of succeeding. Not you providing for me, but me being able to provide for me and mine as you provide for you and yours.

I earned my Bachelors Degree, graduated with a 3.96 GPA, and received the HOOD award for the College of Health and Human Services, which is the highest award that can be received by an undergraduate. However, I must be brutally honest: the education I received was one-sided, depressing, inadequate, and unfulfilling. Despite those facts, I must keep it real. My major put an extreme emphasis on the ability to write, and my writing skills improved as a result. In addition, many of the classes in my Health Education major required reading and interpreting articles from medical journals, which is not easy reading. My comprehension level greatly improved as well, so therefore my education was not a waste; it was just not what I expected it to be.

Chapter Twenty-two: Vice Versa

In 2006, about a month after graduating with my Bachelor degree, nine and a half years after my last hit of crack, I relapsed. There are several things that led up to the relapse:

1.	I lost my drive to create change.

2.	I had lost a valuable support system, which was my husband. Although we didn't get along and argued a great deal of the time, my husband was very supportive. We had been broken up over two years before I started using crack again.

3.	I was living in a drug-infested environment.

4.	After two years of thinking my marriage could be salvaged after separation, I got into a brief relationship with someone who sold crack. I slowly but surely let my guard down and became more accustomed to being in its (crack's) presence.

5.	I forgot who I was and what crack did to me and my community.

6.	I got a job that put me in dope houses, and I witnessed behavior that I had not been in the company of.

7.	I never dealt with the childhood issues that are mentioned previously in this book.

8.   I was out of touch with God.

After leaving this drug for so long, it was very hard to handle the crack cocaine high. Many things came up for me. I was barely sane under the influence this time. Prior to relapsing, I had become extremely close with my fifth child, Andre. We went everywhere together; that lasted until I had a hit of crack cocaine, which made me unable to face him. I also had a new tweak that was added to my high. I would imagine that one of my children were being raped somewhere.

My father's actions had finally come back to haunt me after all of these years; the ability to not be able to trust my own flesh and blood, the man who was supposed to protect me, played out during this relapse in a way that could have gotten me locked up. I was on super high alert for my children's safety and was on standby if I had to kill someone for violating them sexually.

It is weird how my childhood came back to haunt me much later in my addiction, but I am glad it waited until I was a lot older. Otherwise, I probably would be sitting in prison with a life sentence for something that I imagined was happening to my children. I never received any type of counseling as a child, and I was not even considered to be the real victim because I wasn't the child who had to have a baby, so I was expected to cover my pain. These feelings that I had about my children being molested were a very dangerous problem/tweak because I was ready to kill someone at the drop of a hat at the thought of my children going through that. I didn't realize that I was stuffing that much pain.

This notion was very intense. Not only was I afraid for my children sexually, I was afraid for myself sexually. There was something constantly bothering me that I couldn't see. Crack was a very spiritual experience for me, or shall I say it put me in touch with an evil spiritual world that was out to take my mind. This may sound crazy to some and may be written off as mere hallucinations in the medical world. However, I heard voices and experienced many things that I cannot truly say were unreal even now that I am in my right state of mind. It may have been unreal to people who are not living a foul, immoral lifestyle, but those voices that keep us insanely addicted are real to the addict. The only way I was able to keep my sanity was to convince myself that I was in keen touch with evil spirits under the influence of crack, something I still believe at this very moment.

Although I am still struggling at this very moment to get back on my feet, I believe my relapse was a very valuable experience. If I had not relapsed, I would still not know what the most pressing issue in my own community was. I would have believed that the issues that are concentrated on in the public health academic setting are the top priorities for the Black community. They don't have a clue. Twenty some-odd years later, crack cocaine remains one of the biggest problems in the Black community. The crack epidemic is not over; it has just branched out and had babies named the killing epidemic, the dropout epidemic, the foster care epidemic, the gun epidemic, and the incarceration epidemic. Since its invention, many of us are dead, locked up, or spiritually removed from the community, with crack cocaine as the underlying cause.

Nothing has changed as far as the availability of the drug is concerned, so the war on drugs was unsuccessful. Or perhaps it was successful at creating a needy group of people who will constantly fund California's largest industry, the correctional industry. The California Department of Corrections and Rehabilitation has close to a ten billion dollar yearly budget. Drug offenses are the leading causes of people going to prison. And only the Lord knows how many people have gone to prison for drugs indirectly. This is big business, and despite the correctional industry, we have social workers, case managers, lawyers, judges, drug dealers, counselors, surgeons, and countless others whose livelihoods depend upon crack addiction and thus are able to thrive because people such as myself become enslaved. Crack cocaine has become a vital part of America's income. Although people of all races are affected, the Black community is where it is openly peddled and thus is the hardest hit. We are and continue to be the front line soldiers in this drug war.

There are companies who have profited and continue to profit undocumented dollars in the crack game. I can remember one day we were sitting in the crack house after I had relapsed, and we decided to hold a mock trial. I was the prosecuting attorney, one of my crack cousins was the defendant, and another one of my crack cousins played the judge. We decided to take Arm and Hammer Baking Soda, Bic lighters, and

Brillo to court for participating in drug activities and profits. Here is a snippet of the trial.

I was playing the role of the prosecuting attorney representing the Black community: "Mr. Arm and Hammer, you have been in the crack business for over 25 years. Without you there would be no crack cocaine. You are the only difference between powder cocaine and crack cocaine. Because of using you, people receive more time in jail. What do you have to say for yourself? When are you going to give back to the Black community?" My crack cousin who acted as the defendant Arm and Hammer responded, "I do not make anybody do anything illegal. I am not responsible. There are many other uses of my product." Another crack cousin who was sitting in the mock courtroom then shouted out, "You ruined my life!" We all started laughing.

My crack cousins felt it was also necessary to prosecute Bic and Brillo for profiting in the crack game and consumer fraud for altering the lifespan of their products after the invention of crack cocaine. Bic lighters and Brillo (Brillo is used to make a screen for the pipe) used to last a lot longer prior to the crack epidemic. This trial may seem far-fetched, but it is not too far off base. Too many powerful people are benefiting from the use of this drug, and thus it is not given proper attention. When is the last time you heard about crack on the news? According to Wikipedia, the crack epidemic ended in 1991. If that's so, would somebody please notify the people in the projects that the Emancipation Proclamation, Jr., has been signed, and we are free to go on with our lives?

I would also like to mention that this drug was successful at getting to the Black community's secret weapon, the Black woman. I was raising four children on my own, without one father present at the time when I relapsed. I didn't realize what part I played to my family until after the relapse. My house was well organized and most of my children were grown when I relapsed, but the absence of my spirit left my house looking like Hurricane Katrina had hit.

The loss of respect to the women in the community who use this drug only leads to further destruction of the community. It is time to love her; she is the backbone of the community; embrace her. It is obvious that she is very powerful, or we could go on without her. It is no coincidence that the killing rate has gone up in the Black community since the invention of this drug. Who does a young man have to confide in if his momma, grandma, or auntie are not available?

When I relapsed this last time, I was extremely angry and fighting on almost a daily basis. However, the last altercation I had made me think about where I was headed if I didn't stop, which was back to prison. There was a lady who constantly picked on me and called me a crackhead bitch whenever she saw me. One day, I was tired of being bullied. This woman called me a crackhead and said, "Bitch, don't have me get up out of this car and whoop your ass!" She said this while she acted as if she was trying to get out of the car. Her window was all the way down while she was doing this, so I knelt down and reached way back and socked her between the eyes with all of my might.

I wasn't about to let her get out of the car and do anything to me. I was beyond that stage in my street life and addiction, and anybody who knows me will tell you I usually hit first, especially if I feel threatened. To be honest, I am too scared and too little to let somebody hit me first. I had enough of being abused, so it was do or die with me. After I socked her, she started holding her head and moaning, "Ooooooooooooohhhh!" When she got her composure, she started hitting her boyfriend who was in the car with her and blamed him for me hitting her. She told him, "You let this bitch hit me!" He then got out of the car and pinned me up against the car.

One of my crack cousins was looking out of her front window, and I asked for her to call my son Dominique to get this man off of me. The woman then made a broadcasted announcement out of her back window: "Dominique's momma is out here fighting!" She repeated it three times. The next thing I knew, a crowd of people came running around the corner to my rescue, a group of children ranging between the ages of 6 – 19, being led by a local prostitute with whom I had became very close, who was wearing a baseball cap on her head turned sideways. When the crowd that came to rescue me saw what the man was doing to me, the children began to chase the man; he wound up getting hit by a car while he was running. By the grace of God, he wasn't too hurt because he got up and started running again.

The children kept saying he got hit by the car on purpose, but that didn't sit right with me. I also couldn't understand why this woman that was talking so much mess about me never got out of the car. I expressed my confusion with one of my crack cousins, and she replied, "She didn't get out because she can't get out." Come to find out the woman was a paraplegic. I asked them, "Why didn't anyone tell me she couldn't walk?" They responded, "Because she does that to people all of the time; that's what she gets!" Not only did I cause someone to be hit by a car, but I also socked a paraplegic with all my might in the head. I went home within the next couple of days because I didn't want to hurt anyone, and most importantly I didn't want anyone to get in trouble trying to protect me.

Things were different for me this time around. I had a lot of more respect in my community than I did when I first started smoking. I started smoking crack at the age of 20; I was now 43 years old. I had aged out of the game, and I had paid my dues. People in my community loved me and would hurt and possibly kill somebody for me. I didn't want that on my conscience. Plus, the way they were willing to protect me made me think of myself differently, so I went home and detoxified. I slept for a couple of weeks until I felt anxious and tempted to use crack, and then I began writing this book to give me something to do to pass the time away. The more days that went by, the less I craved for crack.

Unfortunately, there is no happy ending to this story. The title of this work was supposed to be From Crack to College; there was no Vice Versa. It was supposed to be a success story; however, I am now aware of the fact that when my community is not successful, neither am I. When I relapsed, I gave up on the notion of this book, but I have come to the realization that my relapse adds drastically to the story. Otherwise, the role of crack, the co-star of this story, would have been underplayed.

Today, as I mentioned previously, I am struggling with staying clean. I would like to go back to school in the spring to pursue a Masters of Art in Adult Education. Although I am still very passionate about health disparities and social justice issues, I cannot and will not stomach the white folks' version of attacking these issues, so I have decided to go to the root cause of poverty and health disparities, which is a lack of education in many cases.

I have been recruited by the community college I graduated from to teach a non-credit health course to people who have been court mandated to participate in self-help classes through Proposition 36, a drug offender rehabilitation law. In my class, we discuss all of the issues that I was taught while pursuing a higher education, but we do it in a manner that fosters innovative thinking and hope, emphasizing to the students that there is a chance at beating the tremendous odds against eliminating these disparities.

It is ironic that this career path has been chosen for me. But if you paid this story any type of attention, it was in my blood all along. Maybe this is why I was so turned off by the education I received. I believe I can do a much better job at promoting innovative and hopeful thinking when it comes to addressing some of the issues I learned about. I have a lot of knowledge in the field, passion and experience, but I still have factors that complicate my success, which are my addiction and environment. Nevertheless, I am glad that I am blessed with the ability to keep trying; some folks are not so fortunate.

Chapter Twenty-three: The Plea

After I wrote all of this down I had to figure out what I wanted a reader to get from my story, and there are several people that I am speaking to. Just in case you miss the message that is there for you indirectly, I have decided to spell it out directly. The first message is for academia. Your concentration on Black folks is not fully representative if you don't tell your students about our amazing ability to bounce back from adversities. Your curricula lacks hope and therefore will most likely turn out students who lack faith. Change cannot take place without someone first having faith that it will happen.

I've always wondered why a lot people in the social service/public health field tend to be very dry and rude. It may be due to the fact that the training they received about the issue or issues which led them to get into their field was not delivered with a sense of hope and helped to put out the fire which was put there to fuel their particular battle. The focus of public health is supposed to be equity, but your students are not taught to want for their clients what they would want for themselves: equity.

Furthermore, I understand that the odds are the so-called underprivileged people who are the center of your curricula are not likely to be present among your students, but what if they are? You have unknowingly excluded their presence from your curricula because you are not expecting them, and thus if they happen to show up, your message can be offensive because it is one-sided. One of the main focuses in public health is to help empower the communities that are experiencing health disparities to make changes for themselves. Empowerment is another word that is commonly used in the public health academic setting. Shouldn't that also be a focus in the classroom? If you can't exercise this type of treatment in your classroom with your students, then what you are teaching is hypocritical and mere lip service. If you don't know how to empower Black students, learn how.

The next message is for the Black community. We need to come together to find some solutions. I have never witnessed a protest, health fair or demonstration aimed at fighting this long-lasting enemy, CRACK COCAINE. Are we going to just throw in the towel before we've launched a real fight? We are the strongest of the strong. We have capabilities to survive despite insurmountable odds against us once we have tapped into that inner strength. It is time to pull out those strengths and talents to help those of us in need.

Don't give up on your people who you have lost to this drug. That is part of the plan. If you count your family members and loved ones who suffer with a crack addiction as merely worthless crackheads, our community will remain separate. Instead we have to come together to figure this thing out. Let's pray for them. There is nothing that we cannot beat if we put our minds to it. We must fight against this as a people. If we do not change the way we are dealing with this drug and its devastating effects, it will never receive the attention needed to help reduce the damage that is being and has been done because it is not one of their concerns or priorities.

How long will we have to endure this burden? How long will we be targeted? How long will we be silent? How long will we not realize that the absence of the people who are killed, addicted and locked up for this drug is a great loss to the power in the community? How long will we not realize that the sale of this drug limits us for the rest of our lives due to the risk of being incarcerated and getting a record that is NEVER forgiven? How long will we overlook the fact that we are seen as the expendable population? How long will we (those of us who are addicted to or sell this drug) work for people who want us dead? How long will they be able to snare us with the same trap? How long will we accept what is unacceptable?

It is unacceptable that so many young Black youth have turned to this drug for an income. It is unacceptable that we parents look the other way. It is unacceptable that we have nowhere to turn to. It is unacceptable how available this drug is to us. It is unacceptable that we must carry all of this weight. It is unacceptable that we have lost so many people. It is unacceptable how many of our children have to suffer.

The last and most important message is to Black people addicted to crack cocaine all across the country. I know what you are going through. You are not alone. You are not imagining things. It IS a conspiracy, and the cards ARE stacked against you. You have been set up and surrounded with lethal weapons, AKA drugs, alcohol and guns. It may seem hard, but you can tippy toe around these vices.

Don't be dismayed; the good news is you are amazingly strong; you can win. This entire drug war is in your hands because it is funded by your actions and choices. Now reach down in your soul and fight back! Do not give up! I wrote this so that your voice could be heard because **YOU ARE SOMEONE SPECIAL WITH A SPECIAL PURPOSE, AND THAT IS WHY THE COMMUNITY HAS NOT BEEN THE SAME WITHOUT YOU! WE NEED YOU! WE MISS YOU! WE LOVE YOU!**

Chapter Twenty-four: The Update

It has been awhile since I wrote the majority of this book. When I began writing this book, I had been off of crack for a couple of months; it has now been almost five years. So many things have happened since I wrote this book; I thought it would be unfair to not give a brief update. At the age of 43, I gave birth to my 6th child, Kingdom Barack, who happens to be autistic. I obtained my Masters degree in Adult Education. We have a Black president, Barack Obama. I bought and lost a four unit building, and I also lost my teaching job due to the Great Recession, and my mother and my grandmother have both passed away. I realize this may be a lot to throw at you in just one paragraph, but just imagine how much it has been for me.

Yes, I am still struggling, but I am nowhere near where I came from. I wish that I was ballin' out of control by the time I wrote this, but unfortunately I am not, and it is time to put it out anyway. This is not a fairy tale with a happy ending; this is true life. Due to my criminal history, race, gender and environmental factors, I have to face many levels of discrimination, and it is extremely hard for me to find someone that is willing to give me a job that suits my level of education and intelligence. I am not writing this for anyone to be discouraged. I am writing this, so that perhaps people who are in power will give us, meaning formerly incarcerated people who have been deemed public enemy number one because of our indulgence in the crack game, a chance to excel. The criminal justice system has broken America's bank, and it is time for those of you in power to keep open minds while considering those of us with criminal records for job opportunities. How will we ever stop if you don't give us a chance to?

Would you be comfortable with living below adequate standards for the rest of your life? I think not. I can't be either, and neither can many other people like me. If you want to change the incarceration epidemic, it is time to change policies. Furthermore, those of you like me who have had your abilities to soar limited by your past endeavors no matter if it was something you did yesterday or long ago, you can make it happen. Just get beyond the guilt and do it. Please be advised that if enough of us get educated, there will be enough of us in power to make a way for each other. Therefore, we need each other.

Our ancestors didn't give up to slavery, and we cannot give in to modern day slavery. It has been 15 years since I was released from prison, but it doesn't change the fact that I am automatically eliminated from many opportunities because of my past. Society has conveniently chosen a spot for formerly incarcerated people in the employment arena, and that spot is represented by entry level, menial jobs that tend to lead us back to where we came from. I have six children, and regardless of my past, I still would like to leave them something besides a public housing unit when I die, and I would like to do so legally.

Although my higher education has not paid off financially in the time frame I thought it would, and I'm still waiting on the BIG BREAK, my education has paid off in other areas. As I mentioned previously, my comprehension level is much higher than it was before I became educated, which makes me much more capable of reading through malarkey, AKA bullshit. I am also better equipped to speak up on behalf of myself, my family, and my community. I cannot give up because I know that I am in a much better position crack-free and highly educated to be discovered by powerful people who have an open mind for my capabilities. I have to hold fast to the notion that everybody in power is not foul because I know that ultimately God holds all power.

My grandmother once asked me, "How many lives do you have?" I was perplexed by what she said, and I responded, "What do you mean?" She went on to say, "I've never had as many chances as you have had." When I think about it, I realize how many times I should have been dead. I cannot count the number of chances I have received. For some reason, I am blessed with a strong spirit that is unwilling to give in despite the odds. Many people who have engaged in the activities that I have engaged in cannot forgive themselves. Guilt is a stagnating emotion. I make mistakes, but I have to get over it or die. It's that simple.

Being that I am still standing and was blessed to wake up this morning, I have not run out of chances! Therefore, I can't stop and won't stop! The BIG BREAK is inevitable! It is up to me to prepare and make sure my next moves are my best moves. I realize this may not be the outcome you expected. If you feel cheated, wait for the sequel. IT AIN'T OVER YET!!!!!!!!!!!!!!

The Bonus Rounds

I have written a few poems to deal with the situations I have faced and the choices I have made. I am including them as bonuses for my readers.

THE BACK DOOR

I thought if I followed by your rules that you would play fair,
I fooled myself into believing that you could actually care.
But I stand reminded of who I am, a child of the Sun,
And realizing that in most cases it is Your will that be done.
I was very disappointed when I was disallowed entry,
Into your magical world that's withheld from so many.
You are in charge and hold keys to the front door,
But you withhold access to the colored and poor.
All of a sudden I remembered just who I am,
The capable one, "OH YES I CAN!"
There is an entrance that is unguarded and greatly underestimated,
Because it requires humility and patience, the entrance is not gated.
My ancestors went through great lengths to show me the way,
Through the entrance that will give me hope today.
It is the entrance used by the colored and poor,
It is the omnipresent, almighty back door.

ACCEPTING MY CALLING

Why do I feel the need not to comply?
To hold my head to the ground and not look to the sky?
I have been blessed with the ability to know right from wrong,
And identify areas that prevent us from growing strong.
Why I am uncomfortable with following my gut,
And speaking on behalf of mine who are currently in a rut?
My spirit is ready and has been thoroughly conditioned,
But my flesh is in doubt and does not give undivided attention.
There are issues that do not speak true to my soul,
These issues prevent us from coming together as a whole.
Although I have the privilege of being able to discern right from wrong,
I am afraid to sing out this almighty song.
Please give me the strength to be guided by faith and not by sight,
And the wisdom to bite my tongue in order to promote what is right.
I've known my plight for quite a long time,
But it is against the grain and requires help from the Divine.
"Why me, my Lord?" my flesh feels the need to ask.
"Because you received undeserved mercy, this has been designated as YOUR task".
"But there are so many people who could fill my shoes."
"When you find them let Me know, and I will give them the rules."

A LETTER ADDRESSED TO THE 99%
(WHAT PERCENTAGE AM I?)

At what point did I become included?
If you make a difference in this country, will I then be excluded?
When your actions create change, will I still be considered a part of the pack?
Or is that when you will remember that I am Black?
Will you finally give me that 40 acres and mule you've been hoarding?
Or are the people of the Sun the one's you'll be avoiding?
How long have you cared about me?
Why have you not helped my community?
I beg to differ, and I would like my percentage to be reclassified.
By the way you treat me; tell the truth, so I can be dignified.
My options and choices are limited because of who I am,
The traps that were set and Nature's hands.
Racism is real and is carried out by the MASSES,
Disguised in false beliefs and stretching out among ALL classes.
In a country where Black folks are being warehoused like slaves,
How can you expect me to join you when I am in a daze?
As a matter of fact, I would like to be removed from your roster,
At least until you learn to treat me fairly you imposter!

CPSIA information can be obtained at www.ICGtesting.com
Printed in the USA
LVOW05s1358210314

378414LV00011B/101/P